Mrs. M. B. Caldwell:
From her Husband.
June 17. 1870.

LESSONS AT THE CROSS.

LESSONS AT THE CROSS:

OR

SPIRITUAL TRUTHS

FAMILIARLY EXHIBITED IN THEIR RELATIONS TO CHRIST.

BY

SAMUEL HOPKINS.

WITH AN INTRODUCTION,

BY

REV. GEORGE W. BLAGDEN, D. D.

EIGHTH EDITION.

BOSTON:
GOULD AND LINCOLN,
59 WASHINGTON STREET.
NEW YORK: SHELDON AND COMPANY.
CINCINNATI: GEORGE S. BLANCHARD.
1864.

ADVERTISEMENT.

The following papers were written at different times, and without any reference to each other. I gather them from a multitude of others almost at random, and in their original form; making a little volume which, as *such*, has no pretensions to unity. Consequently, similar aspects of some particular truth occasionally recur in illustration of different, but analogous, subjects; which in a consecutive work would be a faulty repetition.

If, however, I secure the Christian sympathy of the reader, and conduce to his spiritual profit, a few imperfections of method or of style will not interfere with my chief object in the issue of these pages.

S. H.

January, 1852.

CONTENTS.

		PAGE
Introduction	. . . .	ix
I.	Spiritual Life, — its Nature and Method .	9
II.	Spiritual Life, — its Growth . . .	27
III.	Daily Faith in Christ	42
IV.	The Conditions of Salvation . . .	63
V.	Peace of Mind	77
VI.	Divine Grace commensurate with Man's Necessity	85
VII.	Religious Despondency	99
VIII.	The Excellence of the Knowledge of Christ	116
IX.	The Wealth of the Believer	154
X.	The Recognition of Christ's Grace, — a Duty	185
XI.	The Believer's Debt to Christ . .	222
XII.	Service the Requirement of Christ .	238
XIII.	The Results of the Christian's Afflictions	253

INTRODUCTION.

The manuscript copy of this volume has been submitted to my perusal; and I have been animated and strengthened in my own religious principles by reading it. It is, perhaps, a fair inference, that others who peruse it will be equally benefited. It is luminous with Christ; and therefore it may be conscientiously and unreservedly recommended. In some cases there may be found expressions which the reader would not desire to adopt as his own. Possibly, too, in some instances, an eye that looks for any thing like theological flaws may be able to discover something to expose. But it will find Christ; and that object may well draw away its vision from any real or imaginary defects. Why should we not read, and be delighted, to find Him; and be little concerned whether it shall please Him to come to us in the bright and glorious raiment of the Mount of Transfiguration, or in the garments in which He walked over the hills and valleys of Judea?

But this book needs no apology. It is well and naturally written. No Christian can read it without being helped by it in walking the strait and narrow path. With its comprehensive view of the extent of the *grace* of God in Christ Jesus I have been particularly pleased; while its whole tenor is such as to make it wear the appearance of one who comes to the Christian pilgrim as he is wearily treading through the "wilderness of this world," — like Greatheart, in the beautiful allegory of Bunyan, — to inspire him with renewed courage, and cheer him on in his way. We want words of cheer, in this our devious journey. Amid the ponderous theological works that some of us may read, and the philosophical views of religious truth in which we may love to indulge, we are in some danger of becoming too theoretic and cold. But a practical work like this quickens our somewhat languid feelings, and strengthens us in doing the will of God.

I have spoken of the prominence it gives, in one or more of its chapters, to the comprehensiveness of the grace of God in Christ Jesus. It extends the influence of this grace to the blessings we receive from the works and providence of God, as well as to favors essentially spiritual.

Are we not in some danger of failing to notice this, in the distinction we very properly make between providence and grace? And on account of this failure do we not lose something of that glow of gratitude and felt obligation for the multitudinous blessings we receive from God, that we should otherwise experience? Do we not ask with less fervor, "What shall I render unto the Lord for all his benefits?"

The close connection there is between God's dispensations of providence and grace, — including, as I would wish to do, for my present purpose, in our idea of his ways of providence, his works also in nature, — is so intimate, that we may make continual use of one of these departments of his blessed government in illustrating the other. Particularly may we thus use His works of nature and ways in providence, to illustrate the revealed truths of His grace.

We know that this is continually done, to some extent, perhaps, by all who "believe that God is, and that he is the rewarder of them that diligently seek him." But may it not be done more intelligently, as well as constantly, than it has been done, by many of us? And with the Bible as our guide, may we not use them in a more positive form, for the enforcement of religious truth, than many are accustomed to do?

Butler has used the analogies between them, with great power and success, to answer objections to the general truths of revealed religion. And the Rev. Mr. Barnes, of Philadelphia, has shown with much clearness and force, in an interesting and able review of

Butler's immortal work, that the principle of his reasoning may be happily employed in replying to the objections often urged against each one of the principal doctrines of Evangelical religion.

But may we not make more use than we have done of these analogies, in positively illustrating these doctrines, as well as in answering objections against them? and this too without running into any of the extravagances of what has been called "spiritualizing" every object and event, without any regard to Scriptural authority for doing so?

I shall not attempt to introduce here any examples of the forms in which I think this might be done; inasmuch as this notice is only introductory to what is before the reader, in a volume written by another; and in performing such a service it would be inappropriate to present any particular sentiments or theories of my own. Let me only, then, call the attention of some of my fellow-travellers through time to eternity to this little work; and venture to introduce it to them, as to a fellow-passenger, who, judging from my own experience, will both help and encourage them on their way. Meanwhile, as allusion has been already made to the beautiful allegory of John Bunyan, it may not be amiss to take leave of the reader, in the last line of his own "Apology for his Book":—

> "O, then come hither!
> And lay" this "book, thy head, and heart together."

G. W. B

LESSONS AT THE CROSS.

I.

SPIRITUAL LIFE,—ITS NATURE AND METHOD

THE vague ideas which, it is to be feared, prevail respecting spiritual or eternal life are dangerous. They are hurtful. Oftentimes they are fatal.

Many think themselves in the high-road to heaven who would at once see that they are in the road to death could you divest them of their false ideas of what heaven is, and of what spiritual life is. Many a darling hope of heaven would explode, like a child's bubble, if the false disciple of Christ should only see what spiritual life is. Many a proud worldling, now wrapped in false security, would tremble like an aspen-leaf in the tempest, should he only see what spiritual life is. Many a man would find his refuges of lies crumbling over his head, if he only saw the palpable, eternal contrariety between spiritual life and his own every-day demeanor. And many a Christian, now half fed, faint, and sickly, would put on gladness and beauty like a garment, had he a distinct, living, abiding perception of the mode and nature of spiritual life.

He who thinks that it is merely a state of enjoyment after death, is wrong. He who fancies it to be a state of enjoyment to which nothing but the power, the love, and the grace of God are necessary, is wrong, — absurdly wrong. He who views it as a state of enjoyment which may be secured merely by the deeds of outward obedience, in conjunction with God's power and love, is also absurdly wrong. He who thinks that it is a state of enjoyment for the inheritance of which faith and repentance are needless, or necessary only as the terms of an arbitrary stipulation, is wrong. And such wrong views lead to corresponding errors in one's every-day course; to self-delusion; to false consolation; to false confidence; to false hope; to eternal death.

By Life, we understand something more than the perfect organization or structure of that which has existence. We meet with a plant perfect in its parts, but without vital action. It has no *life*. We meet with another which *has* vital action; but the action is impaired, it is weakened, it is sluggish. There is perfect organization, it may be; but there is not *life*, in the full meaning of the word. So the Scripture speaks in reference to the soul; representing men whose souls were in *existence*, and in *action*, as spiritually *dead*.

By *life*, we understand, and so do the Scriptures, the thrift, the *healthy*, *happy*, action, of any thing which has existence. Thus *vegetable* life is the thrift, the well-being, the good or happy state, of the plant. *Animal* life is the thriving, healthy, happy state of the body. When it is *full* of thrift; when its functions are performed without impediment; when its food nourishes; when its senses are quick and keen and true; when, thus, every beauteous and good thing around it is tributary to its enjoyment; and when it seems to inhale enjoyment to the full extent of its powers, — we say it is *full* of life. Death is the consummation of bodily woe; the lowest, most fearful condition to which the body can be reduced. So the *fulness* of life — life being the opposite of death — is the body *full* of enjoyment; the best and highest condition to which the body can be raised.

And thus, too, by *spiritual* life we mean, and the Bible means, something over and above spiritual *existence;* something over and above the soul's perfect *construction.* By spiritual death, the Bible does not mean, that the soul ceases to be; nor that it has ceased to act; nor that it is bereft of any of its faculties of action. And so by the soul's *life* the Bible does not mean merely that the soul is existing; or that it is acting; or that it is endowed with ability for all action; for all this is comprised in that condition which the Bible calls the soul's death. Something more than this, then, is distinctive of the soul's life. In one word it is — *happiness.* When the action of the soul is a happy action; when its thoughts are happy thoughts; when the impressions which it receives from external objects are gladsome impressions; when its affections are happy affections, — then the soul has life. And when *every* successive thought, and action, and impression, and affection, is happy; when *every* truth and event and object upon which it looks seems clad in beauty; when nothing can come in to darken, or affright, or ruffle it, — that is *fulness*, perfection, of life, because it is *fulness*, perfection, of enjoyment.

But more. This life of the soul, when it exists in renewed man, is enduring. Adam had originally spiritual life in its highest degree. So had the angels who left their first estate. They sinned, and thereby their spiritual life became extinct; spiritual death succeeded. But wherever this life is found among men since the Fall, it never expires. That it can expire, — that true happiness *may* cease, and cease for ever, though the soul's existence never should, — is true. The soul's existence can — at least for aught we know — come to an end; but — it *never will.* And so the soul's life, or happiness, can come to an end; but — it *never will.* We know that we shall exist for ever, because God declares it. And we know that, if we once have spiritual life, it will endure for ever, because God declares *that.* He says, that it is life *eternal.* He declares that he will maintain it, so that, although it *can*, it never *will* fail.

But if spiritual life is the happiness of the soul, then it is not necessarily something which pertains only to a future state of being. Its perfect happiness — *fulness* of life — may not be found here; but its happiness or life in some measure may be, and *is*. It is as capa ble of happiness to-day as it will be to-morrow, or after the death of the body. It has the same capacities for enjoyment, the same faculties of perception and of joyous action, now, that it ever will have or ever can have. It is perfect in its construction, perfect in its endowments; and thus it can be no more *capable* of life in another condition, than in its present; no more, in eternity than at this moment. Its life may *begin* here, and does, and without any alteration of the soul's construction; though that life is matured and perfected only in heaven. And so says the Bible. "God hath given us" — hath already given us — "eternal life." "He that hath the Son *hath* life." "He that believeth on him that sent me," says our Saviour, "*hath* everlasting life, ... *is passed* from death unto life."

But we have said very little about spiritual life, or that life of the soul which is eternal, when we have said, that it is the soul's happiness. The question comes up, What *is* the soul's happiness?

The immortal spirit which has enslaved itself to the body; which has sold itself to serve the body's appetites and pleasures; which, as the Bible expresses it, "walks after the flesh," — has its petty pleasures, its mongrel delights; but is it happy? The man who tasks body and mind, who devotes his highest, his immortal energies to the toils, the anxieties, the perplexities of getting wealth, has his moments of pleasure. But has he happiness? The deluded man who is spurred along through the highways and by-ways of gayety and frivolity, of fashion and dissipation, has his hours of laughter and wild intoxication. But has he happiness? He who drinks at better fountains; who finds his highest wish answered in the quietness and brightness of his own fireside, in the unchecked outgoings of his heart there, has his pleasures. But is he a happy man? Is he satisfied? In each of these cases, — is it well with the soul? Is it fed? Is it thriving? Is it at peace? Has it life? Has it no sensations of famine, — of faintness, — of dissatisfaction, — of disturbance, — to which it finds no antidote?

No; these sparkling fountains of pleasure do not give life. The soul may glean up many good things along its pilgrimage. It may taste many transient sweets. And yet it may have no happiness, no life, no earnest of immortal bliss.

Spiritual life is — the soul acting according to its law.

The whole universe is subject to laws. The system of worlds is subject to laws. If these laws are observed, the beauty, the order, the harmony, the well-being, of the whole are preserved. If these laws are disturbed, the balance of the system is gone, and its utter wreck ensues. Every tree and plant is subject to laws. If they are fulfilled, vegetable thrift and life are the result. If those laws are not fulfilled, sickness and death follow. Animal existence is subject to laws. Every pain, every disease, every disturbance, is because those laws, in some respect, are disregarded. The body is so made that it cannot maintain ease and enjoyment, if its several functions are interrupted. Every infringement of its laws brings evil. It was made to find happiness only in their observance; and without that observance, it cannot find happiness.

The soul also is subject to law. It is designed to act according to the law. It is *so made*, that, if its operations accord with its law, it is happy. To observe its law is its *only possible* method of happiness. Every woe springs up out of its deviation from law; just as the plant springs up from the seed; just as the fruit springs forth from the branch. Every deviation from its law brings woe, just as surely, just as necessarily, as a deviation from the body's law brings the body's woe. This is because the soul is so made, or constituted. Lawlessness is its death; obedience, its life, its happiness, — necessarily. It is going contrary to nature; it is doing violence to itself; it is disarranging, upturning, confounding, its own elements, — when it is acting contrary to its law. We might as well expect the body to live beneath the waves of the sea; the flesh to glow with pleasure in a furnace; the heart to pulsate full and gladly under the knife, — as to expect the soul to be happy while disobeying its law. Let its thoughts go forth as *that law prescribes;* let its will acquiesce in that law; let it act as it was made to act, — then, and only then, is it happy. Its happiness is just as dependent upon its right action, as upon its existence. Upon its acting as it was made to act; upon its loving what it was made to love; upon its serving what it was made to serve; upon its confiding in that in which it was made to confide, — the soul's happiness is as dependent upon these, as upon the will, the power, the love, or the grace of its Creator. If you are going wrong; if you are loving, confiding, hoping, willing, in defi ance of your law, you must change your very spiritual constitution, and thus adapt it to some other law (which is absurd); or you must change the method of your spiritual conduct; or you must for ever die, — you must be for ever a stranger to spiritual happiness. When its affections move in accordance with its law, the soul moves in beauty; it moves in harmony; it moves in peace; and thus to move is life. When they do not, then it "is like the troubled sea when it cannot rest, whose waters cast up mire and dirt." It is in tumult. It is in tempest. And this is — death.

But what *is* the soul's law? *How* was it made to act?

To devote its powers and affections to God. To exist in the steady and affectionate perception of God. This is its law. This is the mode in which it was made and fitted to employ its powers. This is its life. This is its happiness. It must have God, or it dies. It must perceive God as he is, and put forth its chief affection toward him, or it is a fountain of sorrow to itself, — a sea of tossing and tempest, — a chaos of terrific elements, — a sapless branch broken from the vine of its nativity, — a wandering star darting from its orbit and speeding on to the blackness of darkness.

God is the soul's life; God loved, God adored, God as the focal point of all its outgoings, God as the centre, the end, of all its affections. For God, the soul was made. For the enjoyment of God, all its powers were framed and fitted. With its eye open to the affectionate perception of God; with all its affections harmonized, balanced, sanctified, by God's will, — it is *full* of life. It is full of happiness because it responds and moves, looks and loves, according to its law. It is full of happiness because it is full of God.

But God is known only through the Son. "No man knoweth the Father but the Son, and he to whomsoever the Son will reveal him." Christ is the manifestation of God. "The knowledge of the glory of God is given in the face of Jesus Christ." There — is "the brightness of the Father's glory." There — is "the express image of his person." There — is the true God. There — is eternal *life*. "Christ is the bread of life." What food is to the body, such is Christ to the soul. "He that hath *the Son* hath life." In the outgoings of our souls to him, — in our affectionate perception of his excellence, — in our eager searchings into his glory, — we find life. We have been constructed for this; in every part and member. Our spiritual vision is adapted to *that* beauty. Our spiritual appetite is ordained and proportioned to *that* bread. Our affections are dependent for satisfaction upon *that* fulness. Turn away from Christ as the supreme object of our love, and we perish. "He that hath not *the Son* hath not life." Turn toward him as the central point of our affections, and we live.

Would you see what is spiritual life in heaven? Would you know what is happiness there? Would you learn what *makes* heaven? *There* — Christ is the manifestation of God. *There* — he is the brightness of the Father's glory. *There* — he is the bread of life. Saint and angel are looking upon "the throne of God and of the Lamb." Their love goes out to Christ. Their confidence is in Christ. Their song is of Christ. Their life, their bliss, their heaven, is — Christ; Christ, in the fulness of his glory; Christ, all glorious with redeeming love; Christ, all grace; Christ, all gracious to their praise and love. The soul there has — life. The soul there has — Christ. The soul there has its life *in* Christ; attuning its affections to his will; bathing itself in the fulness of his glory; and drinking of the waters which flow from beneath his throne.

So the soul *here* that lives, lives upon Christ. Its happiness comes from him. It is made glad in proportion to, and by, its perception of him. Its chief joy is the ingathering of his excellent glory. Its subordinate joys are the quiet, peaceful movements of its subordinate affections according to the will and pattern of Christ. Its life is sustained in the closet by its "fellowship with the Father, and his Son Jesus Christ." The spring-tide of its life is when it seats itself beneath the cross, and looks at the amazing glory of the Godhead in the sufferings of Redeeming Love. Its richest, purest joys are when it is so filled with its views of Christ, that it longs for an angel's harp and a seraph's tongue to celebrate his praise. *This* — is Life. And this is life which outward troubles cannot touch. This is a tide of bliss which worldly adversity and poverty and bereavement only swell to a higher mark; because they impel the sufferer, with the more eagerness and thankfulness and closeness, to Christ; because they impel him to fresh and larger draughts from the fountain of Christ's sympathy, fellowship, and love.

Happiness is the right action of the soul toward Christ. Where this right action is, there are ten thousand thousand streams of happiness flowing in upon it. Wherever, and in whatever, it discerns any trace or interpretation of Christ, it gains a foretaste of heaven. Every memento of him, — every proof of his power, his presence, or his love, — whether in the Word, in the doctrine of Atonement, in the election of grace, in the typical ordinances of the Gospel, in the events of providence, or in the beauty and bounty of nature, — is a tributary stream of blessing. It is a drop of "honey out of the Rock." It is a fresh draught to a thirsty soul from "the spiritual rock that followeth him, and that rock is Christ." It is a taste of "angels' food." It is a gleaning of the manna of heaven. "He that hath *the Son* hath life, and he that hath not the Son of God hath not life." "Except ye eat the flesh of the Son of man, and drink his blood, ye have no life in you. Whoso eateth his flesh and drinketh his blood hath eternal life. For his flesh is meat indeed, and his blood is drink indeed."

This is the method of spiritual life; this and this only. Thus spiritual life is not mere enjoyment. It is the soul enjoying *Christ* in the exercise of its affections toward him. It is the soul acting as it was *made* to act; the soul letting out its affections toward Christ *rightly;* putting the seal of Christ's proprietorship upon its every member, upon every affection, upon every power. *Perfect* life, perfect bliss, is the movement of *all* its powers, in unison with its law, around "the brightness of the Father's glory," perfectly, truly, unceasingly. There every thought and every affection and every passion, every object and event and truth, is tributary to its happiness; because the water which Christ gives is within it "a well of water springing up into everlasting life."

This consecration of the soul's powers, this employment of them, is the law of our conduct, the method of spiritual life. But this law is not something which God has devised to show his sovereignty withal. This law, that the happiness of the soul shall be found only in affectionate intercourse with Christ, is not something which God has ordained merely because he pleased to ordain it; or because of our peculiar condition as sinners; or because he could and had a right to make such terms of life with us sinners as he had a mind to make. No such thing. It is our law, because we are constituted as we are; because it is the only mode of happiness, the only mode of spiritual life, *possible* for creatures with such endowments as ours; because it *must be* our law while we remain in respect to our spiritual constitution as we were made. And it must for ever be our law, because our endowments and our wants can never be changed. Circumstances will change. Situation will change. Every thing to which change is possible may change; but the soul's relation to Christ, never; the soul's dependence upon Christ, never; the soul's high-born faculties, and its tremendous necessities, never, — never. This law is the soul's law everywhere; on earth, in heaven, in hell, in time, in eternity. It is man's law. It is the saint's law. It is the angel's law. It is the law of all. Obeyed, it yields life. Disregarded, it yields death, — death to the deathless soul.

The life of the soul cannot be sustained except by the right exercise of its affections heavenward, Godward, Christward; therefore it will not do to suppose that nothing more is necessary for us than the forth-putting energy of Divine love, power, grace. Something more *is* necessary; as much so as what there is in God. "He that *hath the Son* hath life. He that *hath not* the Son of God hath not life."

The life of the soul cannot be sustained except by the right exercise of its affections toward Christ; therefore to say that warm affections and spotless honesty toward our fellowmen will insure our salvation, is absurd. "He that hath not *the Son of God* hath not life."

The life of the soul cannot be sustained except by the right exercise of its affections toward Christ; therefore for the Christian to think to find enjoyment, or to be clad in beauty, or to bring forth fruit, or to glorify God before men, while his eye is riveted elsewhere than on Christ, is absurd. "He that *hath not* the Son of God hath not life."

The life of the soul cannot be sustained except by the right exercise of its affections toward Christ; therefore to suppose faith and repentance to be merely terms upon which God has arbitrarily stipulated to make us happy, is absurd. "He that believeth on the Son *hath* everlasting life, and he that believeth not the Son shall not see life, but the wrath of God abideth on him." "This *is* eternal life, *to know* the only true God, and Jesus Christ."

Is it irksome to you to think of Christ? Do you let out your best affections somewhere else than toward him? Do you find no spiritual refreshment in praying to him? in reading of him? in hearing of him? in seeing him in the atonement, in the sacrament, in the events of his providence, and in the works of his hands, — in the moon and the stars which he has ordained? Then your soul is wrong,— all wrong; not only guilty, but *acting* wrong, — acting in defiance of its very law. And because so acting, and *in* so acting, it is all disarranged, — it is all upturned. You are doing violence to your own soul; using it as it was never made to be used. You have "no life in you." You are dead, — plucked up by the roots, — withering, famishing, fruitless, joyless, hopeless. You are going down to your grave all unfit for heaven; all ripening for the *second* death.

II.

SPIRITUAL LIFE,—ITS GROWTH.

We never can enter heaven unless our souls are spotless. We must bear the *perfect* image of Christ. "Every thought must be brought into captivity to the obedience of Christ"; every motion of the affections must be in exact accordance with the law and will of God; every disposition to do wrong must be slain; every feature of the inner man must be just like an angel's, just like Christ's,—or we shall not enter into rest; we shall surely lie down in sorrow. We must first "come unto the measure of the stature of the fulness of Christ." There must be glory upon us like Christ's glory. There must be beauty upon us like Christ's beauty. There must be perfectness within us like Christ's perfectness. We must be "without spot or blemish or any such thing."

No truth is more clearly revealed in the Bible than this.

Heaven is the soul's *perfect* happiness; and heaven is the soul's *perfect* holiness. There is no heaven without a perfect likeness to Christ, any more than there is heaven without perfect happiness. And this is so, not because God has said it shall be so, but because he has made us such that it must be so. It is so, not merely because God must disconnect happiness and sin, or else wink at sin; not merely because he must deny heaven to the imperfect in order to be consistent as a governor, — an administrator of law; but because perfect holiness is *essential*, in itself, to perfect happiness; and that, too, irrespective of Divine consistency. There is necessity for perfect holiness as a condition of heaven here, — *here*, — in the very wants and capacities of the soul itself. Hence the necessity of moral renovation to those who are "dead in trespasses and sins"; the necessity of turning about from the lawless misuse of our faculties to that use of them for which we were made; the necessity of becoming "new creatures in Christ Jesus." And inasmuch as the sinner is "*fully set* to do evil" with his faculties, *hence* the necessity that this moral renovation, if effected at all, be effected by the Holy Spirit. There must be a beginning of holiness. There must be a beginning of resemblance to Christ. There must be a beginning to that life of the soul which is by the birth through the Holy Spirit, as well as to that natural life which is by the birth of the body. There must be a *first* right emotion of the soul Godward and Christward in order to spiritual life, as well as a *first* filling of the lungs, or a *first* throb of the heart, in order to the life of the body.

But the commencement of spiritual life is not its perfection. That exercise of the affections toward Christ which constitutes the life of the soul, does not constitute fitness for heaven. Love to Christ is not always perfect love. Resemblance to Christ is not always perfect resemblance. There is a wide difference between spiritual life in heaven, and spiritual life on earth. There is a wide difference between the joy which fills the heart of an angel, and that which first beats in the heart of a new-born soul on earth. A difference not in kind, but in degree; not in nature, but in strength, in vigor, in fulness. But all this difference must cease. The intermediate ground between the holiness of the new-born convert and the glorified saint must all be passed over. The babe must "come unto a perfect man" before he can stand side by side with the patriarch or the angel above.

The difference between spiritual life and spiritual death is this, — when *dead*, the soul's affections are employed without reference to God's law. The man loves what he pleases to love, and as he pleases to love; he does what he pleases to do, and as he pleases to do; without stopping to ask, — "What is God's will?" "What is right?" "What is wrong?" "How has God made me?" "For what has God made me?" He just throws himself upon the objects around him, and loves them, and serves them, and *lets alone* the objects above him, —God, his Creator, his Saviour. *Alive*, the soul lets out its chief affection to Him who made it; asks for God's will, for God's glory, for God's law, in the direction and in the measure of its emotions; loves what God pleases it should love, and strives to love *as* God pleases it should love. *Dead*, it so directs and proportions its affections, that it gathers as many sorrows as it does pleasures, as many griefs as it does delights; it so behaves, that it is dependent solely upon the restraints of Divine grace, and upon the mushroom objects of this present state, for its *present* exemption from perfect misery. *Alive*, its efforts to control its affections aright are efforts each tributary to its happiness. So far as it succeeds, so far it finds happiness. All its emotions which are in accordance with its rule of action are heavenly and blissful, — its emotions toward God, its emotions toward the world.

Its first efforts are feeble. Its first delights are feeble. Its first efforts are imperfect, — very, very imperfect; and so are its first delights. The first outflowings of its love toward Christ, though they may flash and sparkle like the mountain spring in the sunbeam, are but a little rippling stream; though they may leap and bound with gladness, they are still small; though they may seem clear as crystal, and all-beauteous in their pureness, yet they are shallow and of a span's breadth. But as they go on, they swell; they deepen; they widen. They may have less of sprightliness, but they have more of strength. They may have less of clearness, but it is because they have more of depth. In other words, spiritual life is progressive in this respect, — the love for Christ is becoming stronger and stronger; the heart is devoted to him with more fervor and with less fluctuation; its affections toward earthly objects, — towards wealth and kindred, — are becoming more chaste and heaven-like, and tranquil; "the issues of life," the conversation, the conduct, are more and more like Christ's. Of course spiritual enjoyment is proportionally augmenting; the enjoyment of Christ is more and more; the enjoyment of Christ's outward blessings is more and more; and thus the soul goes on from obedience to obedience, from love to love, from grace to grace, from strength to strength, from gladness to gladness; till it gets the victory over the last corruption, attains to spiritual maturity, wakes up in the *perfect* likeness of Christ and to "fulness of joy."

There are slips in the Christian course. There are sad, sinful, shameful relapses from the onward, upward tendency of spiritual life. There are many wanton and presumptuous exposures to temptation, which bring their cursing blights upon the soul's holy growth, and shroud it in darkness, and buffet it with tempests. But still it advances. It recovers what it has lost, and then rises to higher holiness and richer joys. By and by, it becomes steadfast in its love; perfect in its efforts; perfect in its glories; perfect in its enjoyments; ripe for heaven. But it reaches this point, it surmounts the world, it gains the summit of perfection, it ascends unto fulness of joys, *step by step.*

The little bird, just fledged, flutters from its nest with chirping and gladness. But it must warble many a solitary, broken note; it must take many a blundering, devious flight from bush to bush, from field to field; and then, it can go upwards; then, it can wing its way straight and strong; then, it can utter its song rich and clear. So the soul, just brought into "newness of life," must make many an effort in unpractised weakness, and glean up many imperfect and fluctuating joys, and sing many a broken, faltering note, ere it can be attuned fully to the new song, matured to the stature and strength of an angel, and able to "mount up with wings as eagles."

But I drop this course of thought. I have said enough preliminary to my object. Let me (will you?) take you aside, my Christian brother, and whisper a word or two in your private ear in reference to what I have now stated.

Are you a weak and trembling believer in Christ? Is there a feeble, fluttering motion of spiritual life within you? Does it sometimes seem good and reviving to you to get a twilight perception of Christ's excellence? *so* good that you long for the full disclosures of eternal day? Does it seem to you that you would like to twine your affections strongly, steadily, upon him? Yes. There is sweetness to your ear in the sound of his name. The mention of his love quickens the beatings of your heart, and the light of your eye. Your emotions towards him are *sometimes* discernible and happy. But they are *so* faint, *so* few, *so* far between, — they are *so* different from what they should be, that you point to these very feelings as witnesses against yourself. Yes, you are affrighted because you lack the vigor, the completeness, the sympathy, of spiritual manhood. You sit down to look at the feeble, fitful affections of your heart toward Christ; you sit down and mark the great difference between yourself and what you ought to be, — the vast difference between yourself and those who have "sat at Christ's feet" for years, between your knowledge of Christ and theirs, — and you are frightened.

Frightened at what? Because you are not strong in faith. Because, *as* you are not strong in faith, and strong in hope, and strong in spiritual joys, it seems to you that you have *no* faith and *no* hope and *no* happiness. You argue, that because you are weak, therefore you are dead; that because you have not yet been able to point to your own abundant fruits, therefore you bear neither blossom nor bud; that because your joys have not been strong and rich and steady, therefore you have no union to

Christ, — no spiritual life at all. Why! my brother beloved, your reasoning is a babe's reasoning! Your judgment is a babe's judgment. You talk and think very like a babe in Christ Jesus; yes, — I repeat it, — like a babe in *Christ Jesus.* You admit, — you cannot deny, — that there is something like *attraction* between you and Christ; some faint yearning within you to go and "sit at his feet"; some feeling like this,— that you would love to hold communion with him if you dared, or if you could, or if you knew how to, — that it would be to you a sweet privilege to discover his excellence and love if you might. . . . . . What *is* all this within you? What is it but the infant motion of spiritual life? What is it but the fruit of the spirit? Would the natural heart, would the man "dead in trespasses and sins," sigh for the perception of Christ? Never; never. Therefore I say, that, if those feelings are your's, you are a babe *in Christ.* But *you* infer, that because of their littleness you have no ground to hope that you "have passed from death unto life."

Let me tell you, — infancy comes before childhood; childhood, before manhood. He who would become a saint in heaven must first be a babe in Christ. The beginning of spiritual life is always infantile, weak, unsteady, small.

Is it right, is it rational even, for you to suppose that the new-born child of God should, at the first pulsation of spiritual life, overleap all the weakness and timidity of childhood, and stand forth at once in all the strength of perfect manhood, — "in the measure of the stature of the fulness of Christ"? Is it right, is it reasonable, for you to suppose that spiritual life of a day's duration should be as strongly marked as that of a year's duration? that that of a year's, or of three or five years' duration, should approach as near maturity as that of "an old disciple"? Is it reasonable for you to say, that, as you have not the spiritual vigor and the spiritual comfort of one who has been long in Christ's school, therefore you have none? Why! it is just as though I should find a stripling of half a score of years trembling under the awful apprehension that he had none of the elements of manhood, because, forsooth, he fell short of manhood in stature, and strength, and wisdom. Surely, the only comfort I could give him would be to tell him that he *was* a child, — a foolish child indeed; but a very child, pushing upward, day by day, to a better stature and a better understanding. The only comfort I could give him would be to tell him that he *was* a child; and that in his *childhood* was his hope and promise of manhood.

And so I would tell *you*, my brother. The smallness of your affection for Christ is the hope and the promise of maturity in Christ. The feebleness of your faith is the groundwork of a strong faith. The faintness of your spiritual perception is evidence that you see. The tremulousness of your spiritual enjoyments is an earnest of eternal life. Spiritual life is progressive. Therefore its beginnings must be small, and weak, and imperfect, and fluctuating.

Again. Is there within *you*, my brother, a little, feeble outgoing of your affections to Christ? a little, feeble effort to conform yourself within and without to him? a little, feeble measure of delight as you think or read or hear of him who died for you? a little, feeble warming of your soul as you seek him betimes in your closet? How came these things there? Who gave them birth? What are they? The least such feeling within, — be it so small even that *you* can scarcely discern it, — the least such feeling within you is of the work of God. It is the feeble beginning of eternal life. It is a matter in which you ought to rejoice. It is something which ought to fill you with gratitude. It is something which ought to quicken you to outbursting praise. It is of *grace*. It is of *God.* It is *all* of grace. It is of *pure* grace. It is the budding of spiritual life in the heart of one who was bound and cursed with spiritual death. It is a bow of promise arching over a dark and polluted heart. And for that, — yes, for that imperfect, feeble, infantile motion of your feelings towards Christ, — you ought to utter praise; unblushing, open praise. For that, — little as it is, — you ought to receive the seal of Christ's covenant, and utter the open vow of consecration, and pledge him your soul and body in the cup of the sacrament.

And more. That motion of your feelings towards Christ; that inclination to weep with penitence and joy as you think of his dying love; that melting tenderness of spirit which you sometimes feel toward him, gentle and child-like as it is, — is *God's* work. It is a work of grace. It is ground for hope that you "have the Son of God"; that you have Life. It is the first swelling of a little seed which shall sprout and shoot up and grow unto *perfect* Life. *But* it is a small and feeble, though a precious thing; *therefore* watch it; guard it; cherish it; culture it. Go with it to the mercy-seat. Go with it to the cross. Go with it, day by day, to the closet; that there it may be nourished by your communings, by your tender and tearful and confidential fellowship, with your Redeemer. It is a small and feeble thing to-day; *therefore* take care, — take precious care, — lest something overwhelm it and stunt it to the bitter sorrow of your soul. There it is. *God* has implanted it. Deal well with it, for it is an earnest of his grace; it is the purchase of Redeeming blood; it is the germ of your soul's immortal life; it is the only pledge of your salvation. Spiritual life is progressive. Its beginnings are small and tender. They must *not* be despised. They must *not* be neglected. They must have tender nursing and care. They must be trained and guarded by prayer, by truth, by Christian sympathy, by Christian fellowship, by all — all — the means of spiritual culture. "Work out your *own* salvation, ... *for* it is God that worketh in you."

Once more. Is there within *you*, my brother in covenant, — is there within *you* a little, feeble outgoing of your affection toward Christ? a little, feeble, fluttering pulsation of spiritual life? And how long has it been there? Ten, fifteen, twenty years? What! and is it *yet* feeble? *yet* faint? *yet* small? Are you *yet* a babe? *yet* a babe in your knowledge, in your love, in your hope, in your faith, in the pureness and beauty of your outward life? Shame! shame! Sin! sin!

And *did* you care *only* to be "born again"? *only* to be adopted? *only* to get the signet-mark of salvation? *only* to have a little, weak, infant hope of heaven,—a something that you could turn to and cling to in trouble? Why, "you ought to be a *teacher*, and now you have need that one *teach you* again which be the first principles of the oracles of God"! And, at this rate, when will you be ready to depart? when will you be fit for heaven? when will your spirit be in perfect unison with Christ, with saints, with angels? At *this* rate,—when? Remember, spiritual life is *progressive.* And it has remained in its infancy in you because it has had no nourishment. And it has had no nourishment because *you* have not eaten freely of "*the bread of life*"; because *you* have not lived in close and daily fellowship with Christ; because you have neglected the fellowship of his saints. It is your shame. It is your sin, my brother. Not your shame and your sin, that you have these symptoms of spiritual life, or that you are a babe in Christ; but that you have been a babe so long; that you have not *grown* in holiness, in hope, in faith, in strength, in spiritual happiness. Remember, spiritual life is progressive. You must "come unto a perfect man, unto the measure of the stature of the fulness of Christ." You *must.* You must, or you cannot enter his courts; you cannot see his glory; you cannot wear your crown; you cannot take your harp. Then drop your sin; drop your shame. "Put away the *childish* things" of spiritual life. Give yourself to the work of its culture; so that, when he comes, you may meet your Lord in peace. Make haste, — make haste to ripen for heaven. "The day is far spent." The work is a great work, and it must — it *must* be done.

III.

DAILY FAITH IN CHRIST.

St. Paul was a Christian. He was Christ's. He was the *property* of Christ in the fullest sense, — in a peculiar sense. He was Christ's by *consecration;* Christ's by *service.* He had baptized his every member unto Christ. He had stamped the signet-mark of voluntary surrender to Christ upon every bodily power; upon every power of thought; upon every inward affection. Christ was his Lord, his Master; he, Christ's humble, happy, devoted, steadfast servant.

He had not always been Christ's property in this sense. Once he was "a blasphemer, and a persecutor, and injurious." The life which he once lived in the flesh was against Christ, wholly and bitterly. But the life which he lived when he wrote to the Galatian church was another life. It was *for* Christ. It was *by* Christ. It was *with* Christ. It was *in* Christ. Speaking of himself and his Christian associates, he says: — "None of us liveth to himself, and no man dieth to himself; fo whether we live, we live unto the Lord; and whether we die, we die unto the Lord; whether we live, therefore, or die, we are the Lord's."

Such was the life of the chief of the Apostles. Not a life devoted to himself, or to his kindred, or to the Church; but a life devoted to Christ; tributary to his own good, to the good of his kindred, to the good of the Church, *only* as they were Christ's, — *only* for Christ's sake, — *only* in the way of serving Christ.

What Paul did as Christ's servant, we ought to do. What Paul was as Christ's, we ought to be. The life which he lived, we ought to live. We ought to be as much, as steadfastly, as happily, devoted to Christ as Paul was. Christ has loved us as truly as he loved Paul. He has given himself for us as well as for Paul. We have as truly lived against Christ, as Paul did. And we have the means of sustaining a Christian life, — a consistent, uniform, beauteous Christian life, — as well as Paul. Our obligations are no less than his. Our ingratitude and perverseness have been no less. Our means of grace are no less. Our outward temptations, and our inward corruptions, are no greater.

Paul maintained the consistency and beauty of his course "by faith in Christ Jesus." "The life which I *now* live in the flesh," said he, "I live by the faith of the Son of God." When he bore the taunts and buffetings of the Sanhedrim with a bold, but meek spirit, it was "by the faith of the Son of God." When he stood up alone before the supreme court of Athens, and spake against the religion of their fathers, it was "by the faith of the Son of God." When he made Felix tremble, and woke Agrippa to compunction, it was "by the faith of the Son of God." When he overcame temptation; when he fought against his indwelling sin and against wild beasts in the theatre; when he counted worldly things but loss; when he bore up, under full joy, against the maddened tide of persecution; when he was led to crucifixion glorying in the prospect of a martyr's death, and singing hymns of thanksgiving and victory,—it was "by the faith of the Son of God." *This* was the spring of his Christian life. *This* was the secret of his Christian consistency. *This* was the means of his Christian triumphs. All his devotedness to Christ was sustained by faith in Christ. His devotedness to Christ was an *every-day* devotedness. Of course the faith by which it was sustained was an *every-day* faith.

There is much Christian faith, — true, saving faith, — which is not *in motion.* In other words, there are many (and to their shame be it said) who have been taught of the Spirit to exercise faith in Christ, who have within them the elements of faith, yet are not *believing.* They know *how* to confide in Christ as their strength. They know *how* to confide in his blood of atonement. They know *how* to confide in him as their bosom friend. And they do so confide in him *sometimes;* and sometimes they do not. When they do not, they are believers, it is true; but they are not *believing* believers. Faith exists, and it is a faith which will work; which must work; which will work by love; which will purify the heart; which will overcome the world. But to-day it is slumbering. The man goes forth to his business; he comes across temptations; he feels the irruptions of indwelling sin; he bows beneath the burdens of care and vexation of spirit, of petty and of solemn afflictions; he quivers under the fiery darts of the adversary; he groans under a sense of weariness, and desertion, and spiritual restlessness, and gloom; — but he does not *rest* upon Christ. He does not *exercise* his faith. To-day, he does not gather up his troubles, — his fears, —

his questions of duty, — his dangers, — his sins, — his corruptions, — and spread them all out before Christ.

But a *lively* faith is something more. It is faith — *in action.* It is the heart actually going out towards Christ. It is the eye actually *perceiving* his excellence, his love, his sufficiency, his grace, his glory. It is the soul actually *awake* to its immense necessities as a sinner, to its *every-day* necessities; awake to the precious truth that Christ is *fitted* to those necessities, in all their number, length, and breadth. "He is worthy to be loved. He is worthy to be trusted with any thing, — with every thing. I see his love, his power, his grace, his glory. There they shine, in the firmament. There they shine, in providence. Here they shine in my own existence; in my endowments; in my history. And there, — there, — I see them, in subduing and unrivalled brightness, in his suffering of death. I will seat myself beneath his cross, and look, and love, and trust, and praise. The Son of God loved *me.* He gave himself for *me.* He cares for *me.* Trust him I ought, — I must, — I will, — I do." Such is the language of a *lively* faith.

But it does not stop here. It does not stop with mere perceptions. A faith which sits down to read the love upon the cross, and looks up to praise it, *corresponds* with him who bled thereon. Its perceptions *impel* it. They impel it to *fellowship*. A lively *discerning* of Christ leads the beholder to a lively *confiding* in Christ. And thus when the eye and the heart are open to what Christ is, and to the soul's dependence upon Christ as he is, the believer *believes*. He points to his sins, and trusts Christ for their pardon. He speaks to Christ of his corruptions, and trusts him for the aid necessary to their subjection. He tells Christ of his own weakness, and trusts him for strength. He lays open the imperfection of his services, and yet trusts him for acceptance. He counts over his exposures to sin from the influences of a seductive world, and trusts in Christ for protection. He numbers and describes the troubles and conflicts of his soul, and trusts Christ for support and sympathy. Every matter which is dear to him, every matter of solicitude, he commends to Christ, and leaves with him. Under a *daily* perception of his Redeemer's love, he *unbosoms* himself to him fully. He who sees what Christ is, what he has done, what he can do, what he is willing to do for every individual sinner, has something to *say* to him. He has his tribute of praise and thanksgiving to render. He has his tale of wants, and fears, and hopes, and sins, to tell over.

This is a lively faith; a faith which is *perceiving* something; a faith which is perceiving "the truth as it is in Jesus"; a faith which is *doing* something; a faith which is commending the soul's necessities, without reserve and without misgivings, to Him who cares for it.

But it does not stop *here*. It is a *lively* faith. It is an untiring faith. It is an everyday faith. Every day it studies Christ. Every day it ponders his excellence. Every day it sits beneath the cross. Every day it is *awake;* awake to the fulness and preciousness of the Son of God. Yes; and every day it leads the believer to the mercy-seat; to the place of communion and fellowship with his Redeemer. It never thinks of doing enough in the way of intercourse with Christ to-day to suffice for the wants and emergencies of the soul to-morrow. It never thinks of communing so much with him to-day, that it will not need to return to-morrow. To-day, it spreads out the wants and burdens of to-day; to-morrow, the wants and burdens of to-morrow. It is as much alive to the soul's necessities and dependence, as to the sufficiency and love of Christ. And while it cannot suffer the believer to think that to-day's communion with Christ will answer the purposes of to-morrow, so it does not suffer him to think that he can live to-day on the strength of communion yesterday, or on the intention of communion for to-morrow. A lively faith in Christ reveals our dependence as an every-day dependence. It shows us that our circumstances are shifting daily; that our necessities are changing daily; and that, of course, we have something to commit to Christ daily. It shows us that we cannot steadily progress in the Christian life without every-day ministrations of grace; that we cannot get our every-day ministrations except by every-day fellowship. And thus, while it keeps us awake to Christ's fulness, awake to our wants, and awake to our dependence, it impels us daily to a throne of grace to rehearse our troubles, our wants, our dangers, in the ear of Him who can help us.

A lively faith is a faith moving within us, and moving *us* daily. This is its peculiarity; it moves, it is awake, it does not rest, it does not slumber. It shows us Christ's excellence every day; it draws us into his presence every day. It impels us every day, not only to confide *in* him, but to confide *to* him and to confide *every thing* to him.

But a lively faith in Christ produces fruits It produces the same fruits in all cases. It produces the same *sort* of results in the life of the believer now that it produced in the life of the Apostle Paul.

It sustains the believer in his devotedness to Christ. Paul expressly declares that it was so with him. His was a life of uniform devotedness to the Lord. All that he did, he did for Christ. All that he suffered, he suffered for Christ. Whether he ate or drank, whether he preached the Gospel or wrought as a tent-maker, he did all for Christ. And what prompted him to this devotedness? What sustained him in this, through perils and reproaches and temptations and sufferings? Why, it was his faith; his faith *in exercise;* his daily confiding *in* Christ and *to* Christ. It was his strong conviction of Christ's love for *him;* his daily confidence in Christ's strength; his daily confiding of his wants, his perils, his all, *to* Christ.

And so it is with every Christian disciple. An acting, lively faith will produce the same results in him. *He* will do all for Christ. *He* will labor, and suffer, and teach, and eat, and drink, and go about his daily business, be it in a sail-loft, or in a counting-room, for Christ.

How can it be otherwise? When a poor, guilty, rescued sinner opens his eyes upon the sufferings of the cross, can he help leaping onward in the service of Him who suffered there? When he looks back to the pit whence he has been digged; when he remembers the wormwood and the gall of his spiritual bondage; when he looks upon the cross and can say, as Paul did, and with full perception of the truth, "The Son of God loved *me* and gave himself for *me*," — can he refrain from doing what he can *for* that Son of God? When he *is believing* that he is "bought with a price," with *that* price, can he feel that he is his own? When he *is believing* that he is brought from death to life, from darkness to light, from hopelessness to hope, from the gate of hell to the gate of heaven, — and this, too, by grace, by *that* grace, by the grace of the *cross*, — can he leap amid the eddies of worldly business and forget it? Can he sit down amid the vintage and the olive plants of his own household, and forget who has bought and who bestowed them? Can he *help* conducting his worldly business as Christ would have him? Can he *help* attempering his social enjoyments as Christ would have him? Can he *help* doing all things for Christ? What! a man go away in the morning from the sanctuary of his closet; from a season of close communion with Christ; from a distinct and refreshing perception of redeeming love; from the business of committing his way for the day to the supervision and care and sustaining grace of his spiritual Shepherd, — go away from all this, and then live that day for *himself*, *not* for Christ! What! go from the fountain-head of living water thirsting for the muddy, brackish pools of the world! What! go away from the precious whisperings of a Saviour's love to be charmed by the glittering and chinking of silver and gold! No. That lively perception of Christ, — that lively committal of one's ways to him, — that lively reposing of one's self upon the care, the grace, the strength, the protection, the salvation, the covenant oath of Christ, — is not something which passes off with the shadows and dews of the morning. It controls the believer's conduct, it sanctifies his motives, through the day. It makes him live for Christ. In his getting of gain he remembers Christ. That faith impels him to the simple, but happy devotion of time, strength, property, children, body, soul, all, to the wishes and service of Christ. It must be so. The case needs only to be stated, — the *natural* force of the most sacred, the most impulsive, of all influences to which the soul can be subjected needs only to be apprehended, — and we *see* that it must be so.

But on this point — the productiveness of lively Christian faith — another thought.

Under all the casualties of life, under all the lying and affrighting suggestions of Satan, under the consciousness of ill-desert and indwelling sin to which the believer in Christ is subjected, this faith will make him happy — *in Christ.* The faith of Paul was lively when he was beaten; when he was hunted from city to city; when he was shipwrecked; when he was condemned to crucifixion. And under all, he was happy in Christ. Satan buffeted him; but still he was happy in Christ. He knew that he deserved "everlasting destruction from the presence of the Lord"; he knew that there was "sin dwelling in him"; but still he was happy in Christ. It was his lively *faith* in Christ which made him so.

The same faith does the same thing for every believer. A wordly affliction comes. This faith keeps the eye open, still, to the perception of Christ. And while the believer is surveying his fulness of love, of tenderness, of grace, to this fountain-head he comes. He comes instinctively. He comes, with his gushing heart, for support and sympathy. He has lost a *worldly* comfort; the warmer, *therefore*, is his appeal to Christ for *heavenly* comfort. He draws nearer to him, for now he has more to deposit with him. He has more to disclose, more to ask; and so his hour of fellowship is more full of trust, of earnestness, of gladness. He is shut out from the sunshine of worldly solace and prosperity. Yet is his eye open to the precious love and sympathy of Christ; and to Christ he flees, like a weary bird to its nest; like the way-worn traveller to his couch; like the shipwrecked mariner to the bosom of friends and the comforts of his fireside; the more happy in his place of refuge because of the darkness and terrors and sharpness of his adversity. He sees and feels that all around him "is vanity and vexation of spirit." Yes; and this too he sees, — like a light shining in darkness, — like the gushing of a fountain in the desert, — that Christ is full of riches, full of grace, full of love; that Christ is a treasure for *him*, a treasure "the same yesterday, to-day, and for ever." And thus troubles, afflictions, bereavements, are tributary to his purest happiness through the transmuting influence of lively faith.

In like manner, when Satan mutters about the deceitfulness of the heart, about the multitude of sins, about the conditions of grace, about the few that are saved, a lively faith says, "What if I may not trust my heart? I will trust Christ. What if my sins are many What if there are conditions of grace? Wha if there are few that are saved? I will trust myself with Christ. He has love, and power, and grace, and of each an overflowing fulness. In him I may and will confide. And thus, while the believer *is trusting* in Christ, while his faith *is lively*, he baffles the adversary and is kept in peace. "Thou wilt keep him in perfect peace whose mind is *stayed* on thee."

And so, too, when he looks in upon the startling corruptions of his heart, a *lively* faith still displays the tenderness and sufficiency of Christ; so that *in* him he is the more glad, and *for* him the more grateful, because of the very extent of his sins and the very hatefulness of his corruptions.

If faith in Christ is *lively*, nothing can exclude buoyancy of heart. The *perceiving* of Christ, — the confiding *in* Christ, — the confiding of troubles, of sins, of life, of death, of soul, of all, *to* Christ, — overpower afflictions, temptations, the fear of the law, and the fear of sin.

But yet more; this lively faith in Christ will make the believer a consistent Christian.

It appeals to Christ for strength. It appeals to him for protection from the evil of the world. It appeals to him for grace to surmount and subdue indwelling sin. It casts the soul entirely and boldly upon Christ for protection through the surrounding perils of the hour. It is not the way of our precious Saviour to withhold his help from those who are *trusting* him thus. He never did it. He never will do it. He never can do it. That appeal of a lively faith must be suspended, that cry must cease, that imploring look must pass away, or the grace *must* be given. There is too much love in Christ, too much tenderness, too clear a remembrance of his *own* temptations, too much fidelity to his own covenant oath, for him to withhold this grace when it is thus sought. Lively faith secures it. It is granted "according to the *proportion* of faith." It comes down from above as steadily, as largely, as faith goes up to ask it. He whose faith in Christ is in *exercise* never trips, never staggers, never falters in his course. The charmer may charm ever so wisely; the grace of Christ is his and is sufficient. Snares may be spread ever so abundantly and ever so skilfully, — the grace of Christ guides him. The world may smile, or scoff, or promise, or cajole, but the grace of Christ keeps him; the arm of Christ is under him; the Spirit of Christ is with him; the power of Christ is imparted to him. He may be in the thickest perils, but he is upheld. And for aught the world can do, his visible life, while his faith is *lively*, will be upright and spotless. None can say of him that he breaks his oath; none, that he is false to his Lord.

Besides, a lively faith is a lively perception of Christ's exceeding loveliness. In the eye of faith the glory of Christ is pictured in brighter colors than the fading and fitful beauties of the world. Christ is imaged upon the heart by an *acting* faith so as to eclipse them. The friendship of the world is contemptible in contrast with that of Christ. The loving-kindness of life's best relation — a *mother's* loving-kindness — is tame, is tasteless, is low, is cold, is powerless, in contrast with that of Redeeming Grace. The pleasures of fleshly indulgence are stale, their enticing power is crippled, to him whose lively faith has just led him to communion with Christ, and has just prompted him to thanksgiving for Redeeming Love. With a lively faith, — a faith faithfully portraying Christ's glory, and warming us with gratitude for Redemption, — wherever duty calls we can go unharmed; be it amid ever so many enticements; be it upon a sea of care and business ever so wide or tumultuous.

A lively faith *is* a security against temptation; it *is* a guaranty of a consistent, beautiful, uniform Christian life; because it *appropriates* the sufficiency, the nourishment, the impelling and controlling influence of Redeeming Love.

But methinks some one will say, " This is fancy; this is the poetry of piety. The picture does not tally with facts. It does not answer to piety in real life. It might have been so with Paul. His *was* a life devoted to Christ. He *was* happy in Christ. He *was* consistent as a Christian. The life which he led *was* by the faith of the Son of God. But where do we see such faith producing such fruits now? Are Christians here, upon our right hand and upon our left, steadfast in their devotion to Christ? Are they happy in Christ? Are their lives beauteous with consistency? Where is their Christian zeal? Where their Christian conversation? Where their eagerness for Christian worship? Where their diligent use of the means of grace? Where their spirituality of life? We see them abound in indolence, in stupidity, in worldly-mindedness, in worldly business, in heaviness of heart; but where can we find these wondrous influences which you ascribe to Christian faith?"

And you yourself, my Christian brother, are ready to echo the words and say, — "Where are these wondrous influences? where is *my* devotedness? where *my* joy in Christ? where *my* consistency of life?"

There they are, — *there* they are, where your Christian faith is; laid aside, — out of sight, — asleep, — to all intents and purposes, *gone*. Suppose that you are truly a disciple of Christ, — your faith has gone to rest. You have checked its lively outgoings. Yesterday, — last year, — you believed in Christ. And when you *put forth* your faith, — when you *drank in* the goodness of Christ, — then you lived for him; then you was happy in him; then your light shone; and you labored and spake and behaved like one who belonged to Christ. But now your faith has paused. It does not *move*. And *therefore* you have ceased to produce these precious fruits of faith. Remember, — I have not said that every *believer* is devoted and happy and consistent. I have spoken only of the *believing* believer; of a *lively* faith; of a faith which *is moving* — every day. Your slumbering faith, for present purposes, is trash. *To-day* it is of no avail. And — what is worse — it is not invigorated, refreshed, by its slumbering. Wake it up. Wake it up. Fill your thoughts and your heart with Christ. Come back to your habits of warm-hearted fellowship. Come and seat yourself, *day by day*, beneath the droppings of his blood. Come and study, *day by day*, the wonder, the price, the grace of your redemption. Come, *open* the eye, *open* the ear, *open* the heart, to Christ; and see if you do not recover your devotedness, your gladness, your consistency, your Christian influence. See if you do not regain your power with God and prevail. See if you do not become a daily blessing to those who are bone of your bone and flesh of your flesh, and who are ready to perish in sin. Come, and see if you cannot shame the cavils of those who question the power and the blessedness of Christian faith.

Your heaviness of heart, your spiritual apathy, your deficiencies of life, your fluctuations, are not because you have a lively faith in Christ, but because you have not. They are because you have suspended the heavenly employment of beholding Him who is your Life, and of trusting him,—day by day. Was you *ever* gloomy when your faith was *lively?* Never. It was when you had lost your perception of Christ. It was when you had lost your access to Christ. It was when the heavens were as brass over you because of your—*un*belief.* It was when you did not go and spread out your sorrows to Christ with all the fulness and freeness of whole-hearted trust. Was you *ever* weary of doing all things for Christ, of laboring devotedly for his kingdom and glory, when you was full of a confiding perception of his dying love? Never. It was when you had shut your eye, or turned it away from the cross, and filled it with some other thing. It was not when you was *believing*. Was you *ever* entrapped by a worldly seduction when the excellence of Christ was full in view? when your heart was on fire with your musings about his loveliness and tenderness and truth? Never. It was when, for a day or an hour, you forgot him. It was when you failed to drink deep at the fountain of living waters. It was on some day when you gave your faith a respite.

And how is it with you now, my brother

* The *un*belief of a *believer!* "Lord, I believe; help thou mine unbelief." Mark ix. 24.

beloved? Heavy-hearted, — gloomy, — sleepy — inconsistent, — to-day? And where is your faith? Out of sight. Out of service. Inactive. And *therefore* you go along slumbering and sorrowing and staggering in your course. A life of beautiful, happy, consistent devotedness to Christ is "by the faith of the Son of God." It is by a faith which will show you, and make you feel in your very soul, that he loved *you*, and gave himself for *you*. Look at *this*. Look at *this*. Let your heart move, and leap, and melt away in gratitude and penitence. Let your faith *act*, — *daily*, — and I will venture you in a tornado of afflictions and temptations. Forget this, — fail to get a lively, subduing perception of Christ's love *for you*, — a single day, — I say, a *single day*, — and a breath of wind, which would not move an aspen-leaf, will prostrate you in shame and sorrow and sin. If there come the least trial of your earthly affections, the least form of temptation, you are gone; you are overcome; you are fallen.

IV.

THE CONDITIONS OF SALVATION.

UNLESS the Bible is an impertinent directory in spiritual affairs, it is evident that God has annexed certain conditions to his offers of salvation by Christ. Although they are couched in various forms of language, they may be summarily expressed in two words, — "Repentance" and "Faith."

Yet God has declared as plainly as words can declare it, — he has proved as clearly as deeds can prove it, — that he has no pleasure in the death of the sinner. He has obviated the great difficulty of remitting the penalty of sin and yet maintaining the honor of his Law, by sending his Son to make atonement for us, so that he can justify the sinner and yet be just. These things being so, it seems at first view strange that God should dictate *terms* to those whom he loves; to those for whose sins innocent blood has been shed. It seems a strange thing for a Father, infinite in grace and tenderness, to take advantage of his erring child's dependence and necessity, and *bargain* with him for pardon and loving-kindness. It seems a strange posture for a yearning father to assume, — to sit down over against a child clad in rags and perishing for bread, and *make a contract* with him for food and raiment and home; strange — for such an one to say, " If you will do so and so, I will help you; but if you refuse, I will not help you." And such a course seems passing strange on the part of our Heavenly Father, when he might bless (because of the sacrifice of Christ) without losing one particle of his honor; without abating one principle of his holy government; without repealing one tittle of his Law.

Yet this is the fact, — God *does* propound *conditions* of salvation. Strange, or not strange, — consistent, or not consistent, — God *does* say, that if we accede to these conditions we shall have eternal life; that if we do not, we shall go into everlasting punishment. Let us examine this fact, — Jesus Christ has made an ample atonement for sins, and still God offers salvation *upon conditions.*

The popular notion of salvation is sufficiently correct. Being sinners, we are exposed to punishment, i. e. suffering. If, either because it would be unjust, or because the tender love of God must compel him to preclude suffering, or for any cause whatever, we are not exposed to punishment, then the notion of salvation is absurd. It is a wild conceit. There is no such thing as salvation. But again; being sinners, we are exposed to punishment or suffering *hereafter*. We are not saved from punishment, i. e. we are not exempt from suffering, — *here;* and if there is no danger of our suffering *there*, then there is no salvation *at all*.

If, then, we steer clear of downright absurdity while we talk about salvation, we understand that we are justly exposed to suffering beyond this present life. We do so, because we understand that the salvation which God offers us in the Gospel is *deliverance* from evil hereafter.

The common, and the common-sense idea of salvation, embraces so much as this at least, — a freedom from all suffering after we leave this world; from suffering to which, under the constituted order of things, we are verily liable as sinners. In other words, salvation is eternal happiness *in the stead of* eternal misery.

Now the *conditions* of this salvation are — Repentance and Faith. What connection is there between salvation and the performance of these conditions? To state the question in different terms, — What influence, if any, have Repentance and Faith upon our happiness hereafter?

Watch the influence of any feeling, or of any act which God has forbidden, upon our happiness even in the present life. What is it? Good, or ill? Call to mind your own experience. When you have been angry, when you have been peevish, when you have been envious, have you been happy? If you have ever allowed yourself in any form of vice, have you had a quiet mind? When you have centred all your expectations upon some worldly good; when you have wedded all your affections to some earthly object; have those things so filled your mind, — have they so met, and responded to, your heart's desire, — that you could honestly say, — "I have enough"? Have they so tallied with the necessities of your soul as to quell its cravings and hush its fears? When you have "loved the creature more than the Creator"; when you have devoted your thoughts, and your strength, and your time, and your all, to something here on earth, rather than to God; have you been so void of fear, so free from inward disquietude, so exempt from the rebukes of conscience, that you were a happy man? Did "not *a wave* of trouble roll across your peaceful breast"? Was there no restless craving for something more and for something better? no bitter thought that you and your idols must part? no disturbing consciousness that you was doing wrong — to God?

Your experience, — my experience, — the experience of the world, — go to show, that the allowance of any wrong passion, of any "inordinate affection," is *in itself* evil. Of itself, it brings unhappiness. Here are wants within us which are in no wise met by the things "which perish with the using." Here are susceptibilities within us which are in no wise at ease, while we are tossed with passions, and stimulated by "inordinate affections." Here is a conscience within us which is by no means clean, while we thus depart from the law of God. But this is *impenitence;* persisting in disobedience of God.

Again. Here is a man whose heart rises up against some mishap in his worldly affairs. God has sent it upon him, and he knows it. But he is unreconciled to the dispensation. His mind does not coincide with God's mind. Is he happy? He goes to the Bible. He is told there that "God will work and none can hinder it"; that God controls all things, all men, all hearts, as he pleases; that he "will have mercy on whom he will have mercy, and whom he will he hardeneth." This testimony of the Bible touching God's sovereignty grates upon his ear like a note of discord. It wakens no response of childlike confidence from his heart. God's sovereignty rises up before him, and his will rises up against it. Is he happy? The Law of God is spread before him, with its demand of perfect, eternal obedience; with its commands respecting his most secret thought and wish; with its fearful penalty of death to the soul that sinneth. There it stands. It speaks. It threatens. It presses upon *his* life; upon *his* speech; upon *his* thoughts; upon *his* accountability; upon *his* destiny. He clashes with it. His heart rises up against the commandment, — against the penalty. Is he happy?

There is *God's* law; there is *God's* sovereignty; there is *God's* providence; and they do not meet his views, — they do not chord with his heart, — they do not agree with his will. He cannot *trust* God for a Law; he cannot *trust* God with the absolute disposal of the universe; he cannot *trust* God for the daily dispensation of providence. Hence the disagreement between him and what God ordains. Hence, and hence only, his unhappiness. But all this is — *unbelief.*

On the other hand, we find Repentance and Faith in God closely associated with happiness. In their best estate on earth, they are imperfect. But so far as they exist, they yield the fruits of blessedness.

If we restrain our passions, if we temper our earthly affections, if we regulate our words and our daily conduct according to the rules which God gives us, we contribute so much to our own enjoyment. So far as we feel right and act right, so far we are happy. So far we have peace. So far we have the approval of our consciences. And this is — *Repentance.*

Again, what is more obviously productive of peace and joy than confidence in God? When a man can look upon all the mysteries of providence, and upon all his personal afflictions, with a full, a lively, a steadfast, conviction that He who has dispensed them has done right; when he can say, with the spirit of a child, "Even so, Father"; when he can thus throw himself with a placid temper upon the current of God's dispensations; under the blackest clouds, under the rudest tempest, adrift upon the wildest billows, he is happy. And this is — *Faith.*

When he can look upon the dazzling doctrine of God's absolute, universal supremacy with a steady eye; when he can turn to this truth with an unwavering assurance, that every decree and every decision, that every apportionment, both of Grace and Justice, will be right; when, thus trusting in God, he can acquiesce in every particular of his government; under every mystery, he is happy. All things — *all* things — are done according to his will; for God's will is his, — his will is God's. And *this* is — *Faith.*

And when a poor sinner, in full view of the terrors and strictness of the Law; in full view of his own sins and ill-desert; in full view of his own helplessness; can trust in the promises of God through Christ; when he can *feel* that in the blood of the Lamb there is a sacrifice for *his* sins; when he can thus leave himself quietly with God, and wait and look for salvation; surely this is happiness. Yet *this,* too, is — *Faith.*

When a child of sorrows, overwhelmed with hardships and stripped of earthly comforts, can go to Him who has smitten him and kiss the rod; when he can say, "Though thou slay me, yet will I trust in thee"; when he can find his way to the place of secret communion to recite his griefs and to ask for sympathy; when he can go to the throne of grace for consolation; though his troubles have been like a flood, and the cup of his adversity like wormwood, yet there, in that man's breast, — in that torn and bleeding heart, — peace gushes up like a fountain and the happiness of heaven like a reviving stream. But this is *another* form of — *Faith.*

Thus we find, upon the most superficial reflection, that impenitence and unbelief are the very fountains of spiritual wretchedness. We find also that repentance and faith are the well-springs of spiritual happiness. Now transfer the operation of these different tempers to the coming state of existence. In this life, the passions are in their infancy; in the next, in their maturity. Here, our inordinate affections are checked; there, let loose. Here, our thoughts are diverted, in a thousand ways, from the truths and the government and the Law of God, — by cares, by business, by social pleasures, by the passing events of a bustling world; there, these things will have no place. Here we get but a glimpse, as it were, of God's Majesty, of his Sovereignty, of his Law, of his system of Grace, — "we see through a glass darkly," — but there it will be eye to eye, "face to face." Is it *possible* for you to be happy — *there* — if you are still in sin? Is it possible, — when the revelations of eternity will make your soul as truly naked to your own view as it is "to the eyes of Him with whom you have to do"? Is it possible, — when your "refuges of lies" will all be gone? Is it possible, — when your covering of self-righteousness will be stripped off? Is it possible, — when your paltry sophistries about your own uncleanness will have vanished like the dew — for ever?

If you are unhappy in *one* degree when the wrong feelings of your heart move within you here, under all the restraints of grace, under all the diversions of a busy life, you may be sure that, when these restraints and diversions are gone, and those wrong feelings leap up within you like a giant loosed from his bands, your cup of misery will be full. It *must* be.

If you are unhappy *now*, when you get only a twilight view of the Law, and the Government, and the Sovereignty of God, what will be the measure of your unhappiness *then*, when (the same unbelief in your heart) that Law, and Government, and Sovereignty rise up before you — *ever* before you — clear, and bright, and terrible as God can show them? What *must* it be?

If the whispered rebukes of a conscience wellnigh stifled, — if the transient twinges of a conscience wellnigh seared by abuse, — harrow up your soul *here*, what will be its damning power when it shall recover its might, and its right, and take its vengeance — *there?*

But — should you stand before God a penitent — every thought, every wish, every employment, in *perfect* unison with his will; enmity changed for love; rebellion, for submission, — should you stand there staying yourself upon him in the spirit of a pure and perfect faith, — then, under the cloudless light of his Law, his Sovereignty, his Gospel, you would find Life such as angels have, and blessedness such as God's. Faith and holiness would bind you to God for ever. They would make your will commingle with God's will, as kindred elements commingle. They would open to you the fountains of God. They would yield to you the *full* fellowship of God. And the clearer and the brighter the purposes, the deeds, the justice, the sovereignty of God should beam before you, — the higher would be the influx of your enjoyments, —

the louder the outgoings of your praise. And thus, while the successive disclosures of eternity would wake you to fresh emotions of faith and obedience, gladness would succeed to gladness, — song to song, — Life to Life, — for ever and for ever.

But, if these things are true, then God is *not* presenting himself before you, and styling himself your Father, yet playing with the miseries of your sinful state by presenting to you arbitrary conditions of salvation. He is *not bargaining* with you for the blessings of his grace. He is *not* asking of you something without which he *might* give you salvation. It is not true, that he *might* save you in impenitence and unbelief, but *will* not. It is not true, that he *might* make you happy while you are what you are, yet does not choose to do it. Your sin and your unbelief are to the soul what fire and famine are to the body. They are to your soul what rottenness is to the bones. They are to your soul what pestilence is to health. It is not true that Repentance and Faith are necessary to salvation just because God commands them. God commands them because they are necessary. Salvation is not hampered by superfluous articles of compromise. It is as free as air. "The promise is unto you and to your children." "Ho! every one that thirsteth." "Whosoever will, let him come." "Come unto me, *all* ye that labor and are heavy-laden." *Such* are the overtures of grace. *Such* are the messages of Divine Love.

True, atonement has been made by Christ; an atonement without which there could have been no salvation; an atonement on the basis of which free grace is proclaimed. But that atonement was not more essential to salvation than repentance and faith are. And though it be, that all power is in God; though it be, that he "delighteth not in the death of the sinner"; though it be, that he crieth after you, "How can I give thee up?"—yet it is *also* true, and *as plainly* true, that salvation *cannot* be effected save in the very way which God has prescribed. Power cannot accomplish it. Blood cannot. Grace cannot.

God has done his part. God has done what you could never do. God has provided an atonement. And now he calls upon you, and all, to do *your* part. He calls upon you to do what he *cannot* do for you,—to repent,—to believe. He calls for this simply because this *is Life;* this *is* happiness; simply because the refusal thereof is *itself* death and woe. His conditions of salvation, therefore, are — simply those affections of heart which *constitute* salvation. He offers you happiness on this only condition, — that you *will be* happy.

V.

PEACE OF MIND.

All men seek after happiness. It is natural. It is right. It is duty. We were *made* to be happy. It was the design of our Creator; and, to this design, he has accurately and wisely fitted the various endowments of our souls and the circumstances of our outward condition. That which will contribute to our happiness he approves. That which will prevent it — and that only — he condemns. In seeking, and in making effort, to be happy, therefore, we do but coincide with God. So far, we fall in with one great object for which he made us.

But God, when he framed us, made us to be happy in a certain way. He so framed us that we can be happy *only in* one certain way. And we differ from God, from the law of God, from all the high purposes of God, the moment we pursue any other way.

Most men *do* pursue another way. They want happiness. But they seek it where it is not to be found. They go up and down in life, paying court and tithes and homage to a thousand worldly objects; tossed by a thousand waves; lured to and fro by a thousand phantoms; and then — go down to their graves worn and wearied, disappointed and empty-handed.

We are surrounded by numberless sources of disquietude; that is to say, there is, perhaps, nothing which is not *capable* of making us unhappy. The prosperity and ill-behavior of the wicked may do it. The events of providence may do it. Our sins, — our liability to evil, temporal or eternal, — may do it. God's Law, — his character, — his sovereignty, — his method of grace, — may do it. All these things may excite within us thoughts and feelings utterly preventive of enjoyment. They may awaken within us fear, or anger, or remorse, or some other emotion of a like nature; and thus induce inward tumult, from the lowest point of restlessness to the highest pitch of distress and frenzy.

On the other hand, we *may* look upon these things without disturbance. We can suffer wrong from men without passion. We can meet disappointment and adversity without a single inward murmur. We can part with property and health; we can give up the objects dearest to our hearts; we can bury all our earthly hopes, — without one wish to question or to reverse the decisions of an adverse providence. We can survey the plan of salvation; the pureness and the curses of the Law; the character and the sovereignty of God, — without one emotion of discontent. We can think of our "sins that are past," and of our ill-desert; we can look upon them just as they appear under the clear light of the Bible; we can behold our vileness in its true deformity, our condemnation as sinners in all its terrors, and death and judgment and eternity with all their solemnity, — without fear and without distress. And *this is peace.* This is peace of mind. This is "the peace of God which passeth all understanding."

If our minds are disturbed, what does it avail us that we are surrounded by the countless tokens of our Maker's goodness? If we are uneasy *within*, what to us are beauty and profusion *without?* What satisfaction do we get from wealth, from honors, from power, from the fountains of domestic endearment, while our "souls are disquieted within us"? When we are fretful that we cannot get more; when we are tossed with apprehension lest we should lose what we have; when we are angry at some frowning providence; when we feel this craving of our spirits for something better than the world; when passion heats us; when sins affright us; when conscience rebukes us, — the very cup of our earthly pleasures is dashed with bitterness. We get not half the comfort we might get from the common blessings of life.

But if our minds are at peace, — then we can behold, with open eyes and unclouded vision, the beauties of God's handiwork; we can drink with lively relish at the fountains of domestic endearment. We can *taste* the sweets, we can *feel* the comforts, we can *enjoy* the blessings, which God has provided for us. If we *are* bereaved; if we *are* poor; if we *are* sick; if we *are* despised, — we can find something to enjoy; the good things which *remain* to us are not spoiled; the flowers still bloom, and we can love them; the providence of God is still around us, and we can rest upon it; the Word of God still abideth, and we can rejoice in it.

What if temporal adversity does come like a flood? What if hopes are dashed, and comforts torn away by thousands? If we can say, "Amen"; if we can say, "Even so, Father; *even so*"; if we can look upon the seeming severity of our afflictions without *a doubt* of their fitness or their rightness; if amid all we can "*sing* both of mercies and of judgments"; we are happy — still. And what though it is declared to us that God is our Sovereign; that every event of providence, of grace, of punitive justice, is according to the eternal counsel of his will? What if it does appear, that God will dispose of us, and of ours, and of all things, just as he pleases and only as he pleases? If we have no quarrel with his sovereignty; if we can look with calmness upon all the particulars of his government; if we *acquiesce* in his absolute supremacy; if we can keep our minds *at peace;* we are happy — still. And what if we do discover that we have not yet attained unto perfection either of heart or life? What if we do behold that we have become obnoxious to a law whose penalty is death; that we are speeding every hour to the end of our probation and to the decisions of the judgment-day? If we can see all this without remorse and without terror, if in view of all we can be *at peace*, we are happy — still. And when we come to die, — though we leave behind those who cling to us for support and protection and comfort, — though the question is yet *to be* solved whether we awake to shame or to glory,—though the moment of our departure is the moment when our destinies are sealed for ever,—if we can commit ourselves to God without distrust; if we can thus keep our minds *at peace;* we are happy—still.

Now this is worth more to us—by far—than outward prosperity. It is better than—money. It is better than—adding field to field. It is better than—the esteem of men. It is better than—children,—than princedoms,—than all the world can give. These cannot serve us in the days of our adversity. *This*—can. These cannot uphold us in the times of our souls' necessities. *This*—can. These cannot stay us up, and wake our hearts to melody, when we think of God; of our sins; of our day of reckoning; and when we come to die. But *this*—can.

What *you* want is—peace of mind. You need something more and something better than the feverish exhilaration of mirth; something more and better than the wearying excitement of worldly enterprise; something more and better than a self-righteous complacency; something more and better than wealth and friends. These things can never make you happy. Place your hopes upon them, and you will reap a harvest of bitter disappointment. Search the world over, — there is nothing in it that can slake your thirst; nothing that can fill your desires; nothing that can give you rest. You want *a quiet mind.* That guilty conscience must be purged. Those disturbing passions must be quelled. That restlessness must be subdued. Those "inordinate affections" must be set in order. Those fears about the morrow, — those flashing anxieties about dying and about going into eternity, — must be overcome. The moment your heart rebels against the doings, or the doctrines, or the government of God; the moment conscience upbraids you with unwashen sins; the moment you feel that there is something unsettled between yourself and God; the moment there bursts up within you the conviction of your soul's poverty and nakedness; — that moment you are an unhappy man.

You must have such commotions stilled. You must find peace. Else you cannot find happiness.

I point you, then, to God. *He* can give you peace. He can still your fears. He can take away the sting of guilt. He can keep you quiet under every hardship; in view of all the terrors of a broken law; through all the solemnities of a dying hour.

You need peace to give you happiness. You need God to give you peace.

I pray you, then, go to God. Go, and establish a covenant with him. Go, and begin fellowship with him. Go, and make his throne of grace your daily refuge; his mercy-seat your hiding-place. When perils overhang your estate or your children; when disease and death threaten to dissolve your dearest ties; when false affection blights your hopes; when the burdens of life press you; when trifles vex you, — *go to God.* When you think of your sins; when you feel the motion of your indwelling corruptions; when you fluctuate between hope and fear touching the question of your spiritual adoption, — *go to God.* Go, — and tell him your troubles. Go, — cast your care upon him. Go, — pour out your soul. Go, — like a child to a father. Go, — spread before Him your sins, — guilt, — fears, — burdens, — corruptions, — all.

VI.

DIVINE GRACE COMMENSURATE WITH MAN'S NECESSITY.

THE Grace of God is the chief doctrine of the Gospel. It is the great light of the spiritual universe.

It is not Divine Love simply; but Divine Love going out beyond the abodes of holiness to find recipients for its gifts. It is Divine Love coming with overtures of blessing to the *sinner.* It is the union, or partnership of Love and Justice; in which both blend their glories and unite their influence to save.

That God can forbear, that he can pardon, that he can be gracious, — is our only hope. It is a sufficient source of joy and peace; and of incomparable preciousness. Yet few so interweave themselves with the promises of grace as to attain to the stability and peace which they are designed to impart. Few so far divest themselves of unbelief as to appropriate that spiritual encouragement which grace affords. "All the promises of God in

Christ are yea, and in him amen"; they are sure, boundless, free; yet few partake of them without trembling and feed upon them without restraint. How seldom are doubts silenced, fears quelled, unbelief shamed, and the adversary foiled by the plea which David used,—"For thy name's sake, O Lord, pardon mine iniquity, *for*—it is great."

"Canst thou by searching find out God? Canst thou find out the Almighty to perfection?" Are not the resources of Divine grace equal to the extent of human sinfulness? Are not the supplies of infinite fulness equal to the greatness of human necessity? "Shall not He who spared not his own Son with him also freely give us all things?" Why, then, should our conception of his grace be diminutive? Why should we fear lest our measure of it be beyond the truth?

One principle upon which Divine grace proceeds is, that its own fulness, or sufficiency should be the most gloriously exhibited.

The display of God's grace is not made in the announcement of what he might do, or of what he intends to do. The *display* of grace is made in the *deed* of grace. In proportion to the greatness of its deeds, is the exhibition of its fulness. If its glory shines bright and clear in the pardon of one transgression, how much more when it freely cancels sins without number and of the deepest dye. If, for the purpose of explaining the nature of his grace and its value, God forgives one iniquity, will he not much more and for the same purpose — O thou of little faith! — answer a penitential prayer for the forgiveness of a *multitude* of sins? Will he not, — think you, — when the illustration of his grace is the greater and the more glorious because of the very excess of sin? Indeed, if there is sin too great to be pardoned when pardon is humbly and earnestly sought; if there is a blessing so great that it must be refused, though humbly craved; if a sinner suing for mercy must perish because he is so great a sinner; and if a needy suppliant must be denied because of the greatness of his prayer, — then what is meant by "the *exceeding* riches of God's grace" which Paul so much extols? If these things are thus, what means Paul when he says, — "God hath quickened us . . . . . *that* in the ages to come he *might shew* the exceeding riches of his grace"? If these things are thus, is not grace so reduced in its measure, so circumscribed and trammelled in its operations, that it is palpably inadequate to its great object, — the showing forth of the boundlessness of God's goodness?

"For thy *name's* sake," says the Psalmist, "pardon mine iniquity, *for* it is great." He pleads the greatness of his sin as the *true* reason for its forgiveness. He pleads that the magnitude of sin affords the better opportunity for the more glorious display of grace; that the greater the act of pardon, the more honor to the name of God; and that the greater the sin, the greater the pardon.

In all our reflections upon the economy and principles of grace, we should always keep in view this grand truth, — that in the bestowment of pardon God always has an eye to the most glorious exhibition of his own excellence.

Another principle which uniformly regulates all the operations of Divine grace is this, — that God herein seeks for the fullest exercise of his infinite benevolence.

He delights in the highest good of his creatures; in their possession of that true, pure happiness which results from the consciousness of his approval, and from a conformity to his character. But particularly in the dispensation of good to the *sinner*, — in visiting him with hope, consolation, liberty, pardon, life, — does God find ample field for the operations of a kindness infinite in its exercise and immeasurable in its benefits. And if the exercise of such benevolence is his delight; if this is one object of his grace, — then it is evident, that the greater our need of his favors, the greater is his readiness to grant them. Benevolence finds the widest range in the greatest act of pardon. Ill-desert is not a barrier to the bestowment of God's grace, but the very incentive to its exercise. Wretchedness is the very occasion of his mercies. The greater the sin, the greater his desire for its removal. The greater the apostasy, and ingratitude, and ill-desert, the greater his desire to reclaim and bless. Inasmuch as Divine grace is based upon Divine benevolence; inasmuch as the *only* sphere of its operation is that of guilt and unworthiness; inasmuch as it is an attribute of an Infinite Mind, — we can imagine no debt which it cannot cancel; no sin which it cannot bury; no wretchedness which it cannot relieve; no want which it cannot supply. There is no limit to its greatness; no end to its bounties; no checking of its fulness; no cessation, no weariness, no clog to its exercise. It is an exhaustless fountain flowing forth *for all* who will drink of its waters. It is an infinite good, covering and liquidating an infinite evil, stretching on and accumulating through infinite duration. Thus he who receives its offers in vain, who passes by its streams and forfeits its benefits, must charge the consequences of his poverty to his own pride and his own folly. He can in no wise impeach the excellence, or disprove the sufficiency, of the grace of God.

Now if these two things are true, — that the putting forth of Divine grace is for the purpose of its full exhibition, and for the complete exercise of Infinite benevolence, — then is it sure, that human necessity, which makes drafts upon that grace and gives the widest field to that benevolence, is the very object which God would search out and relieve. So that Divine grace is fitted to human need; and human need is fitted to Divine grace. The principles upon which it proceeds show us clearly, that God's grace and man's need are precisely coincident, to whatever height, or depth, or length, or breadth, that need may extend.

When I speak of man's need, I mean not only his need of Divine forgiveness, but his need of every spiritual blessing. The mere pardon of the sinner is but the preface of Divine grace. It is only the starting forth of a seed which is to *grow ;* which is to grow on earth, and to attain full beauty and maturity in heaven. Divine grace is not completed in the one act of reconciliation between the sinner and God. It seeks to bestow *all* blessings; to dispense alike the most precious and the least. It would reclaim, it would sanctify, it would comfort, it would sustain the sinner. It would transfer him to pure glory in heaven. It would bestow upon him joys without measure and without end.

Thus there is no limit to the bounteousness of Divine grace. And there is no limit to its *bestowment* where the grace is earnestly sought. I say, — where it is earnestly sought; for he who seeks not, desires not; and he who desires not, takes not; and he who takes not the gifts of grace, of necessity *prevents* their bestowment. He *makes* them, to himself, as though they were not.

Though the grace of God is without limit in every case where penitential desire allows of its exercise, yet there only is it extended. To a sinner with *such* a temper it is *free.* When *he* seeks it and importunes for it, it is given in abundance.

But here I would advert again to the peculiar plea of the Psalmist David. At a human tribunal it would insure condemnation, but at the throne of grace it is the only one admissible.

That we are sinners, is *the* argument which appeals directly and forcibly to those very principles upon which the dispensation of Divine grace depends, — the glory of God and his infinite benevolence. It is the plea which calls his grace into exercise; upon which its bestowment depends. It was the plea of David. It was the plea of the publican, through which he "went down to his house justified." It is the plea which prevails. It bears on its front the fundamental truth upon which every petition of *ours* must be based; that truth which is the corner-stone of every provision, of every promise, and every encouragement of grace.

A plea of good desert would be false. It would therefore be in vain, and impious. So far from securing God's favor and blessing, it would excite his indignation. The publican went down to his house justified rather than the Pharisee; "for every one that humbleth himself shall be exalted."

Would we urge the plea that Christ has died for us? A precious, valid, prevailing plea indeed. But for whom did Christ die? What are we for whom he died? Sinners. If therefore we plead the death of Christ for the bestowment of any good upon us, our plea is *nothing* except as built upon the foundation plea that *we* are sinners, — needy, helpless ruined, desperate sinners. When we seek Divine grace, we must present — side by side with the great truth of Redemption — the prominent, essential truth of our *own* guilt and ruin. The influence of Christ's death; the gifts of the Holy Spirit, of pardon, of consolation; the promises; the proffer of assistance; the invitations of love, — all provisions peculiar to the Gospel, — are interwoven with, and presuppose, the cardinal truth, that *we* are — sinners.

If this truth do not qualify our prayers; if it do not burn in our hearts; if it give not urgency, eloquence, and strength to all our appeals to our Father in heaven, we must turn from his mercy-seat without his smile, — without the gifts of his grace. We must *cling* to the truth that we are sinners, — that our "iniquity is *great*," — or we must let go the promises of the Gospel and the hope of eternal life. The argument of our sinfulness is adapted to the character of God. It is a true argument. It is *the* argument which must be urged, — importunately, earnestly, confidently, — or we are undone.

Now if God extends his favor to us, — if he makes us partakers of his grace, — only on the condition of our urging this plea, then our sinfulness, upon which the sense and truthfulness of the plea are based, must be a reason for the bestowment of grace.

Therefore, if the greatness of his iniquity be the sinner's proper plea, if it is itself the reason for the bestowment of grace, and if it creates (as in truth it does) the sole occasion or opportunity for grace, — how can sin, confessed and argued, furnish reason for sentence against the supplicant for grace? The supposition is a contradiction to the very idea of grace, which *depends* upon ill-desert for its exercise,* and upon the plea of ill-desert for imparting its gifts.

If this is true, then the grace of God is coextensive with the sinner's iniquity; for the greater the sin and the greater the consequent necessity, the more power there is in the argument.

---

* Not, however, for its *existence.* Neither the existence of sin, nor the sacrifice of Christ, was necessary to *make* God *gracious.* On this point the common argument for the necessity of an atonement is grossly belied; and, I may say, caricatured.

The grace of God can reach as far as your sins, my Christian brother. It can cover them all, dissolve them all, so completely that no vestige of them shall ever more be seen. It can overreach all your iniquity; it can supply all your necessity. This is the very purpose, the very nature of grace. "Where sin hath abounded, grace much more abounds." Indeed, when you come to his mercy-seat with the spirit of penitence and with the sinner's plea, God does, as it were, challenge you to tell him of your iniquities so great that his grace through Christ cannot cancel them; challenges you to show him *your* sins *greater* than *his* grace. Not that grace furnishes reason for sin. God forbid. But sin furnishes reason for grace.

Since these things are so, I ask you to look at the Word of God, to look at the grand outline of the economy of grace, and say if it is not a sin to exclaim, in face of the Bible, in opposition to the full and generous principles of God's grace, that we may not, cannot, dare not, approach the throne of mercy, because of the greatness of our necessity or the enormity of our transgressions. Such language results from a wicked, ideal limitation of God's grace; from a perversion of the very principles upon which it proceeds. Sinfulness and necessity are the *indispensable* conditions of its bestowment; but unbelief says, that sinfulness and necessity are the reasons for its denial. By this false doctrine many a conscience-stricken sinner has been impelled farther in sin, and shut out from the kingdom of God. By this falsehood Christians have shrouded themselves with distress, concealed the Divine light within them, groped in darkness, taken up with wailings and tears when they ought to have abounded in hymns of thanksgiving, and thus puzzled and bewildered those who have been watching for the correspondence of their lives to the obvious principles of the Gospel.

Perhaps, my Christian brother, you are hardly aware how, when you have proper views of your own sinfulness, you misuse yourself and wrong others if you suffer that sinfulness to eclipse the glorious radiance of the grace of God.

You are often saying, that you cannot rely upon Divine grace; that you cannot importune for God's aid and pardon; that you cannot step forward in the path of duty and responsibility, *because* your weakness, imperfection, and iniquity are so great. Thus, perhaps you restrain prayer, and neglect duty, and shrink from responsibility, and are tossed from billow to billow, as the necessary consequence of your unjust and absurd views of Divine grace. Just as though that grace was contracted, — just as though it was less than your weakness, and unworthiness, and sin!

For your own sake, — for the sake of God's honor, — away for ever with such aspersions of his grace. Come to the throne of grace. Come habitually. Come boldly, trustfully; not with doubting, and misgiving, and halting, and fear. Come *because* you are a sinner, — because you are a *great* sinner. Come for the pardon of your iniquity, because it is *so* great. Come for grace to help you, *because* you are in need.

And then go on in the discharge of Christian duty, and in the joy of Christian faith; trusting in the grace to which you have appealed for all your needed supplies. With such trust, — with such cheering and reviving views of God's grace, — you may go on through temptations, trials, conflicts, duties, emergencies, any thing and every thing, until that grace shall make its most glorious display in your everlasting triumph and joy.

This one, earnest prayer, "Pardon mine iniquity, O Lord, *for* it is great," will procure for any one the free, copious grace of God; that grace which shall guide him to everlasting rest and emancipate him eternally from sin and from sorrow.

But woe unto him who distrusts that grace, and counts it of less extent than his own transgressions.

VII.

RELIGIOUS DESPONDENCY.

TRUE Christians, who have not sunk into spiritual apathy, often yield to a despondency which the Gospel neither warrants, encourages, or produces. Indeed, almost every one who has been renewed by the power of God knows more or less of spiritual depression, of the deep gloom of spiritual darkness. Every one who has watchfully studied Christian experience knows, that the disciples of Christ very often forget his parting injunction, "Be of good cheer"; forget the apostolic injunction, "Rejoice in the Lord always"; forget the encouragements to the Christian life; forget the promises of the Lord; forget the largeness, the freeness, the occasion of Divine grace; forget every thing save obstacles and dangers, enemies and corruptions; and thus give up to fears, disquietudes, and sorrows. How few rejoice in the Lord! How few exult in Divine Power and Grace! How few, in distrust of themselves and with trust in God, boldly defy every spiritual foe till they have passed from conquest to conquest, till they have entered upon eternal triumph and rest! The harps of God's people are too often upon the willows. Their songs are too often faint, if not silenced. Their spirit of praise and joy is too often languid, if not extinct. One day they chant anthems; the next, are cast down in the dust, and abound in lamentations.

Why? Why do not those who hope, and with good reason, that they have been made "joint-heirs with Christ," rejoice in his Redemption? Why is it, that they do not magnify the grace of God? Why is it, that they do not illustrate the worth of his renewing grace by apprehending *joyfully* the truths of the Gospel? Is there any evil from which he will not deliver them? any danger from which he will not protect them? any real plague from which he will not free them? Is there any thing, in the whole range of spiritual truths or spiritual accidents, which they need to fear? "The Lord God is a sun and shield; the Lord will give grace and glory; no good thing will he withhold from them that walk uprightly." He will in no wise cast out any who believe in Christ. He will impose no burdens beyond what they can bear. "Like as a father pitieth his children, so the Lord pitieth them that fear him." He "will redeem them from all their iniquities," "purge away their sins for his name's sake," and bring them unto Mount "Zion with songs, and everlasting joy upon their heads; they shall obtain joy and gladness, and sorrow and sighing shall flee away." Not one of them shall perish.

Why is it, then, that the children of God, the heirs of immortal glory, should be carried captive by the power of fear? Is the Gospel in fault? Is the influence of evangelical truth the cause? Does the Holy Spirit, by his influences, beget despondency? No; the Gospel is "glad tidings of great joy"; "the fruit of the Spirit is love, joy, peace"; the author of salvation is "the God of hope," — "the God of all comfort." He seeks to "fill" his people "with all joy and peace in believing, that they may abound in hope through the power of the Holy Ghost." "The kingdom of God is righteousness, and peace, and joy in the Holy Ghost."

No; the fault is in Christians themselves.

To account for our religious despondency, we are usually told of our neglect of specific Christian duties; of our sluggishness in the Christian life; of our backwardness in furthering the plans of Christian enterprise; of our deficiency in spiritual meditation; of the manner in which we approach the throne of grace. We are assured, and with truth too, that unless we bear ourselves with carefulness and scrupulousness and uniformity in these particulars, we shall inevitably induce darkness and sorrow. These are important truths. But I pass them over with a mere allusion. There are other causes of spiritual gloom which I wish particularly to designate.

One is, limited views of the grace of God.

Every one who has been renewed in Christ Jesus is conscious of his own sinfulness. He looks upon it with abhorrence. He turns his eye upon his own heart, and upon his own past life, and there he sees sin, — sin, — sin. The more he is taught by the Spirit, and the nearer he approaches to perfection, and the more he learns of holiness, so much the more does he discern the evil of his life and the corruptions of his heart. The growth of Christian character necessarily produces a growing conception of the exceeding sinfulness of sin; of its contrariety to God; of its opposition to happiness; of its contempt of threatenings, of entreaties, of obligations, of Grace. Such, I say, is the necessary result of the advancement of Christian character.

Now with all this knowledge of sin, and with the knowledge that we ourselves are sinners, and with the knowledge of what we deserve as sinners, if there is not a corresponding and counterbalancing view of the grace of God *specially* provided for us, then this perception of our personal demerit becomes a necessary and an active source of disturbing apprehension. So far as it goes, here is a proper view of sin. Suppose in the same mind there is a contracted view of the antidote to sin. Suppose it is forgotten, that sin is the very occasion of grace. Suppose it is kept out of mind, that *operating* grace could not exist but for sin. Suppose it is kept out of mind, that as sin rises up in defiance of God and in defiance of grace, so grace rises up the more earnestly in its plenitude and glory to surmount and liquidate sin. Suppose, while sin is beheld as great, grace is considered as small; that while the conception of sin is extended, the view of grace is limited. In such a case, are gloom and heaviness of heart avoidable? While sin stands before the mind's eye in its true, naked, revolting deformity; while we thus recognize it as affixed to ourselves; while memory recites the history of our wrongs toward God; must we not tremble, can we help being affrighted at our own portrait, if we forget that grace is coextensive with sin? if we forget that it is the *very office* of grace to forgive and to cleanse, and that it is the very odiousness of sin which excites grace? Here is a partial conception of Divine grace; a misapprehension of it; a hiding of its glory; a forgetting of its freeness and sufficiency; a wrong view of its very nature and purpose,— by all which it seems other than it is. Thus, when we imagine ourselves to be contemplating the grace of God, we are truly contemplating something else; something not adapted to our necessities. And so we bear up against this overwhelming, yet true, conception of sin, — alone, unsupported. We ponder the blackness of our character, the terribleness of our deserts, without a counterbalancing view of the richness, the light, the consolation, of Divine provisions. Ascribing an unfounded, ideal limitation to Divine grace, we grapple helplessly and hopelessly with the consciousness of our guilt. Can we, thus, bear up joyfully? No;—we *must* despond, we must sink. Worldly pleasures cannot relieve us. Worldly inventions, — man's wisdom, — have no fitness to our case; they have no power to raise us up, to fill us with peace. Yet, let the conception of sin be extended ever so far; let memory rehearse our transgressions with exact fidelity; let the representations of the Bible, the transactions on Calvary, the approaching judgment, the terrors of eternal death, illustrate with all their force the exceeding sinfulness of sin, — if we apprehend the exceeding riches of Divine grace, — if we canvass its nature, its purpose, its occasion, its greatness, its freeness, — *then* we shake off despondency, and rejoice with exceeding joy. Our conception of sin, our consciousness of its aggravating circumstances, lose all their power to depress.

The more we understand and abhor sin, its power, its curse, — the greater will our *exultation* be, when we see the purpose, the fulness, the freeness of God's grace. When, in the light of the Gospel, we behold that grace ready to supply all our necessities, to remove every curse, to shield from every danger, to purge from every corruption, to wash away all guilt, — nothing can depress us, — nothing can rob us of joy.

But another cause of spiritual gloom — and one, I think, but little suspected — is a wrong method of searching the heart; or, rather, having a wrong *object* in view when searching the heart.

Self-examination is a duty. Its purpose is, that we may see "whether we are in the faith."

Some Christians examine themselves by looking at other objects, — sinful objects, for example, — and then noticing what are their feelings towards them; or again, at holy objects, and then noticing what are their feelings towards them, — and *thus* judging "whether they are in the faith," whether they have the affections required in the Gospel.

Others examine themselves by looking in upon *themselves;* and that not so much for the purpose of ascertaining whether they possess Christian faith, as for the purpose of finding what of *evil* may be in them. They do it with the distinct expectation of finding sin there, with the distinct intention of detecting there the forms, movements, and disguises of sin, that so they may guard against and uproot it.

Others, again, scrutinize themselves not simply for the purpose of detecting and eradicating sin, and not simply for the purpose of judging "whether they are in the faith"; but in the hope of finding something *good* there in which they may glory, — being of a different mind from Paul, who "most gladly gloried in his *infirmity*, that the power of Christ might rest upon him." Or they look in upon their hearts in the hope of finding righteousness there in which they may rejoice; being again of a different mind from Paul, who sought to be "found in Christ *not* having his own righteousness, but . . . . . the righteousness which is of God by faith."

The consequence of such examination of the heart is any thing but satisfaction. Its direct and necessary result, if we are honest and faithful in the work, is despondency.

What is there in ourselves? Any thing which should afford us pleasure? Any thing which should be a matter of exultation? Any thing for which *we* are commendable? Any thing of which we may boast? O, no! nothing! If, then, we exclude other objects from view and fix our vision upon our own hearts, we have before us nothing but imperfection, — sin, — the very thing we most loathe. Thus employed, — especially if we are hoping to find goodness within ourselves, — we, of course, experience bitter disappointment; for we find the very opposite of goodness. Can a *child of God* rejoice while unfolding his own heart?

Can one who hates sin rejoice while discovering it in his very self? How can he rejoice at such discovery when he has just opened the door of his heart with the vain, foolish, fond hope of finding something *good* there? No; so long as he gazes there; so long as he ruminates upon what he finds there; so long as he revolves its particulars, and analyzes its properties, and observes its daily influences, and shuts his eye against every other view, — he *must* be heavy-hearted, he must be discouraged; he cannot but cry out for bitterness of soul. It is absurd for a sinful man to look in upon himself honestly, and searchingly, for consolation. We have no right to do so. It is not the object for which we are bidden to examine ourselves. Nor are we told to look upon ourselves *exclusively* for *any* purpose, or at any time. But we *are* told never to turn our eyes away from *Christ.* And when we, so intently and exclusively, and with a purpose so absurd, gaze upon our own hearts, we *do* turn our eyes from Christ. And we thus disobey the Gospel. What wonder, that in the very act of disobedience we are given over to despondency? It is our duty to look to *Christ;* to drink in the delightful displays of his loveliness and sufficiency. When we do otherwise, our spirits must faint, our hearts must ache. We are out of the way of duty. We are away from the fountain of consolation, and joy, and life. We avert our eyes and exclude the brightness of Divine glory as it shines in the face of Jesus Christ. We are drinking at the very fountain of bitterness and sorrow.

What is it which sometimes pours such a flood of light and joy upon the soul of one just "turned from the power of Satan unto God"? The contemplation of himself? No; it is the apprehension of his Saviour. And what is it which always gives the Christian his seasons of joy? In what is his chief delight? It is in fixing his eye upon the excellence, the loveliness, the sufficiency, the preciousness of his Lord; not in riveting his eye upon the realities of his own heart, and tracing out the repulsive features of his own character. Self can afford no satisfaction to the Christian. The contemplation of self can never fill him with joy. There will be no happiness from such a source, even when we are perfected. David said, "I shall be satisfied when I awake" — satisfied with what? — "with *thy* likeness." Think you that glorified saints are vain of their robes? Do they look into the pure fountains of heaven with pleasure merely because they see reflected their own symmetry and glory? What! when all their perfectness is the work of Christ! when their apparel is all borrowed from the vestry of Divine grace! Pure as they are, is self their chief delight? their great source of happiness? their great object of contemplation? Precious as their purity is to themselves, their *happiness* is in Christ. They are happy not only in the exercise of gratitude to him for what they are, but chiefly in the unwearying employment of getting larger and still larger views of his glory. The throne of the Lamb, — the glory that is thereon, — is the grand focus of their thought and their affection. Every mouth is sounding forth his praise. Every eye is dwelling upon his glory. Every heart is panting for his smile. Every foot is pressing with rapturous devotion to be near to him. There, happiness is in perfection; despondency is unknown. Why? Because there all are engaged in contemplating Him who has "redeemed them to God by his blood," and washed them therein. Because there Christ is the *absorbing* object of thought, of love, of praise.

And shall we, — corrupt, imperfect men, —

so far beneath the saints in pureness; we, in whom God's work—if begun at all—is but just begun; shall we be gazing upon ourselves and turning our eyes from Christ? What have we to do with ourselves as means of comfort? or as sources of satisfaction? We have to deal with ourselves only in the way of *culture*. For our model, our glory, our joy, we must look to Christ. If we would be free from despondency, we must let ourselves alone, except as we strive cheerfully, and patiently, to bring ourselves, by Divine aid, into a sweet similitude to Jesus. And this is to be done only by beholding *him*. "We shall be like him when we see him as he is." Every reviving spiritual impulse must be given to us by some fresh emanation from him. Such impulse cannot come from self; from the energy or the contemplation of self. It must be given by imbibing *his* radiance and contemplating *his* glory; just as the tender shrub receives reviving impulse from the light of the returning sun. Sin will annoy us, because it will reside in us, so long as we abide here. But if we look to Christ, trust him, feed upon him as "the bread of life," then sin, with all its accursing power, will prove only like the chrysalis's web which the sunlight penetrates.

It will soon burst. It will soon be cast off Our souls will then rise to heaven in full glory not for the display of themselves to themselves; not for the display of themselves to others; but to be *humble* witnesses to Redeeming Love, to chant for ever their Redeemer's praise, to dwell for ever upon their Redeemer's excellence.

Where is the source of true happiness? In the creature? or in the Creator? In a fountain of uncleanness? or in the fountain of Divine excellence? Here, — in my heart, for me? in your heart, for you? or there, — in heaven? in the perceptible glory of God in Christ? O! it is surely — there; for you, for me, for saints, for angels, for all. God, as revealed in the person of Jesus Christ, — he is the source of all happiness; of all strength; of all excellence. When, therefore, you or I or any other one turns his eye upon self, excluding heavenly objects, each will be constrained to exclaim, "O, wretched man that I am, who shall deliver me from the body of this death!" To this we must necessarily be driven, because we fix our gaze upon that which is odious, *and* in the same act turn away from the only object which can revive and rejoice us. We look upon ourselves, we look away from Christ.

Where, then, is the cause of Christian despondency? Is it the legitimate influence of the Gospel? Is it a necessary consequence of being a Christian? Is it a fruit of the Spirit? Is it a part of Christian life? Is it an essential peculiarity of a Christian? As well might we suppose it to be an essential peculiarity of heaven. No. The truths of the Gospel, and the influences of the Spirit, produce brokenness of heart, hatred of sin, and an understanding of self. But when the Gospel tells of sin, it points also to grace; when it speaks of condemnation, it also proclaims,—"Christ Jesus came into the world to save sinners." And when the Holy Spirit unveils the sinfulness of sin and the sinfulness of one's self,—without exception,—he seeks to direct us, at the same time, to the glory, excellence, and preciousness of Christ; so that, by looking thereon, we may be more and more like him. Even "the Law is our schoolmaster to bring us *to Christ*." And if we do not heed the Spirit of God; if, *while* conscious of sinfulness, we do not also behold and trust in Christ, and are thus cast down,—where is the fault? In the Spirit of God? In the Gospel? In the nature of piety? No; but in our own error of vision; in our misdirected vision. We can only be happy, peaceful, when we *believe*, only when we behold sin *and* grace; only when we look upon self *and* Christ; only when we can commit sin to grace, and self to Christ. Sin without grace is fearful; but even in view of sin we can rejoice, if we behold the exceeding riches and the sole purpose of grace. So self without Christ is a fearful object of contemplation; but self in Christ, and Christ in self, and self lost in Christ,— this is a view in which we may exult. And this is the view which the Gospel (glad tidings) presents.

Learn, then, Christian brother, how to rejoice. Learn how to glorify God in your joy. And, O! cease to bring suspicion upon the Gospel; cease to teach men to look upon vital piety with dread. Cease,—by allowing piety to have its *natural* growth and to perform its *legitimate* work. Cease,—by allowing to the Gospel its proper, uninterrupted influence upon you; by allowing the Spirit of God,—the Spirit of grace,—the Spirit of consolation,— to lead, to guide, to influence you, just *as He would do.*

"So shall your walk be close with God,
Calm and serene your frame;
And clearer light shall mark the road
That leads you to the Lamb."

Learn how to rejoice. Learn to contemplate Divine grace just as it is set forth in the Gospel; to contemplate Christ just as he is set forth there. Though your faith be but an infant faith, yet why be heavy-hearted when there is so much to make you happy in "the unsearchable riches of Christ"? "Though your sins be as scarlet," and rise toward heaven like mountains, yet, O! why be heavy-hearted when there is grace, full grace, free grace, willing grace, grace enough, with God, to cover them all up, to blot them all out? "Why art thou cast down," O believer! and why is your "soul disquieted" within you? "Hope thou *in God*," and you shall then "praise him for the help of his countenance."

VIII.

THE EXCELLENCE OF THE KNOWLEDGE OF CHRIST.

The true knowledge of Christ is an excellent knowledge. The Apostle Paul, who had received "abundance of revelations," and whose judgment in this matter was formed under the special tuition of the Holy Spirit, declares it to be the *most* excellent knowledge. He says, "Yea, doubtless, I count *all things loss* for the excellency of the knowledge of Christ Jesus my Lord." When he wrote these words, he would rather have known Christ, than to have been rich, or honored, or learned, or beloved, or "a Hebrew of the Hebrews"; rather than to *have had* any thing or to *have been* any thing which men naturally esteem. Like Mary, he would rather sit at Jesus's feet, and look up at Jesus's face, and learn of Him who is meek and lowly of heart, — he would rather have had "the light of the knowledge of the glory of God *in the face of Jesus Christ*," — than to have had any other teacher, or any other object of admiration, or the light of any other glory in the universe. "Yea, doubtless," *now* he would say, "I count all things loss for the excellency of the knowledge of Christ Jesus my Lord." "Yea, doubtless," even the splendors of the golden city are nothing to him; and the glories of archangels, nothing; and the discourse of archangels, nothing; and the fellowship and melody of his fellow-martyrs, nothing; and his own crown of glory, nothing; and thrones, and dominions, and principalities, and powers, nothing,—except as "Christ is all and in all." Upon every face and diadem; upon every pearl and precious stone; upon every mansion, and arbor, and fountain in the New Jerusalem,—there is some testimony of Jesus. All things there are bright and beautiful *only because* "the glory of God doth lighten it, and the Lamb is the light thereof." And thus the knowledge of Christ is the charm of heaven; the key to its beauties; the secret of its holiness, of its harmony, of its fellowship, of its happiness.

The knowledge of Christ includes, evidently, *a correct idea* of him.

We must have a correct idea of his *conduct.* We must understand to what trials and temptations he was subjected. We must understand the truth that he went through all without one evil feeling, or impure thought, or word, or act, toward God or toward man. We must understand also that he maintained through all *every right* feeling, and *all right* behavior, in word and deed, toward God and man, from the manger to the cross; and this, too, while possessed of all the susceptibilities and properties of a human soul. In short, we must have a familiar understanding both of his temper and his life as a man; of their wonderful and spotless beauty.

Again, we must have a correct idea of him as "both *Lord* and Christ"; as "Lord both of the dead and living." We must understand that, "all things being delivered unto him of the Father," "all *power* being given unto him in heaven and in earth," he holds the reins of universal government; that the impulses of *his* hand are concerned in every movement and in every breath of the whole creation, in every event of universal providence, in heaven and earth and air and sea. We must recognize his right to homage and faith and obedience, as King and Governor of all things.

And yet more; we must have a correct idea of his *Love*. It is a Love beyond every other Love. It bore him on through persecution and poverty and the hidings of the Father's face and the chastisement of the Father's rod, through the mysterious sufferings of his soul upon the cross where he was hung and smitten and bruised as the sacrifice for sin. It is a Love which has yearned over us *since* the hour when he cried, "It is finished"; through all our ingratitude, contempt, guilt, foolhardiness, idolatry. It is a Love which has *bought* us; — "with *a price*"; — with the price of *blood;* with the price of *more* than blood. It is a Love which has bought for us, and offers to us, — heaven. It is a Love which has bought for us, and gives to us, our day of grace and our means of grace. It is a Love which has given us food, and raiment, and health, and homes, and domestic enjoyments, and each particular blessing which has ever gladdened our hearts and cheered the path of our pilgrimage. It is the Love of a Shepherd, and Bishop, and Friend; ever ready to help us, to strengthen us, to guide us, to protect us, to comfort us. It is a Love ready to befriend us against sin; against the Law; against temptation; against the adversary; aye, ready and *able* and *longing* to do it. It is a Love ever reaching after us, — yes, after *all* of us, — that it may bear our burdens, and carry our sorrows, and dry our tears, and bind up our wounds, be our troubles what they may, — spiritual or worldly, — great or trivial; a Love for *all* who are careworn and way-worn; for all, yea *all*, who "labor and are heavy-laden." It is a Love, — O for a tongue that *could* tell it! O for a hand that *could* depict it! My brother! my fellow-sinner! beloved of Him who bled upon the cross! I am lost, — *lost*, — here! It is a tide which rises, — and rises, — and never ebbs. It is a sea, — "without a bottom or a shore." No line *can* fathom it. No eye *can* measure it. No supplications *can* tire it. No drafts of the needy on earth or in heaven, for time or for eternity, *can* exhaust it. It is matchless; munificent; unsought; unmerited; unlimited Love. It passeth knowledge. It passeth knowledge.

Now, to know *Christ*, we *must* know his Love. We must understand its sacrifices; its condescension; its grace; its fulness; its sympathy; its sufficiency; its *perfect* fitness to *all* our wants.

Yet this is not all that is included in the knowledge of Christ. It is not merely a correct idea of his conduct as a man; of his supremacy as Lord; of his love as Saviour and

Shepherd, and Friend. It is something more. It is a knowledge of him which exists in the *heart* as well as in the head. It is a knowledge which comes from *feeling* what he is, as well as from *perceiving* it.

When we can sit down, with the Gospels before us, and trace out all the particulars of his weary life, — his humility, his gentleness, his meekness, his filial devotedness to the Father's glory, his filial resignation to the Father's will; when we think of his lovely deportment toward the widow and the childless; when we think of him at the grave of Lazarus, among the faint and hungry, among the liers-in-wait for his blood, in the wilderness, in the garden, in the hall of judgment, on the cross; when we *so* look at these things that "our *hearts burn* within us" toward his spotless holiness; we have a clearer conception, a *different* and a *better* knowledge of him than when we read or think of his life *without* emotion.

And when we *so* think of his exaltation to the throne of the Father, that we *feel* that *his* hand is in every event, that *his* authority is prefixed to every commandment, and that *his* power controls a wicked world, we have a clearer perception, a far *different* and a better knowledge of him, than when we think of his supremacy, but do not *apply* it and *feel* it.

So also is the knowledge of his Love. The sinner who looks at his cross, convinced of his own ruin and helplessness; who looks and *feels* the preciousness of that atonement; who looks and *welcomes* it; who looks and *melts* beneath it; who looks and *casts himself upon* it, — knows something *more* about a Saviour's love than is seen with the eye of the mind. So does he also, when his heart recognizes and feels a *Saviour's* love in his daily mercies and afflictions. So also, when he *feels* the Saviour's sufficiency and watchfulness and tenderness as his Shepherd; and his fidelity as his Bishop; and his sympathy and support and peace-giving influence as a Friend in the fellowship of the closet.

Yes, wheresoever and in whomsoever the character and government and love of Christ have touched the *heart*, there is a knowledge to which a mere reader or hearer of the Truth could not attain for ever. Without this, had we the intellectual eye of a seraph and a place under the clear sunlight of the third heaven and the lessons of "ten thousand instructors in Christ" through successive ages, we should not know so much of him as the spiritual babe knows whose heart is just opened to *feel* the mystery of the cross. Our knowledge — ever so correct intellectually — would be essentially void both of Life and of Truth.

But I have said, in concurrence with St. Paul, that this knowledge of Christ is of unequalled excellence or value.

A tree is known by its fruits. If the fruit be excellent, then is the tree excellent. If its fruit be *most* precious, so also is the tree. What, then, are the fruits of this knowledge of Christ? What effects does it produce? Are they valuable? Are they above value? So, then, is the knowledge whence they grow.

Observe the influence of this knowledge upon the several parts of Christian character.

Here is a man who lives daily in view of Christ. His Saviour is the chief object of his contemplation. He loves, in the morning, to betake himself to the study of Christ. He loves to do it through the business of the day. He loves to do it at evening, and in the watches of the night; in the house; by the way; at home; abroad. He is daily discovering some new beauty in his Saviour's character; some new feature of his Love, or his power, or his providence, or his practical holiness. Christ is the companion of his thoughts, the friend of his bosom, the confidant of his doubts and fears and joys and troubles. He is seeking and finding some new interpretation of Christ in all the history and in all the doctrines of the Bible, — in the scenes of Calvary, — in the terrors of Sinai, — in the works of nature, — in the events of providence. In other words, he is living under the light of his Saviour's countenance, under the influence of his Saviour's example, under the sound of his Saviour's voice, under the sweet influences of his Saviour's fellowship. Thus he has that knowledge of Christ which comes from *intimacy*, — from affectionate intimacy; and in this knowledge he grows.

What is the result? The result! Why! man and man do not more surely assimilate under the influence of daily and friendly and long-continued intercourse, than do man and Christ. The spirit and the habits of an affectionate child are not more surely moulded after the pattern of its mother, by whose side it lives and upon whose bosom it is wont to rest and whose virtues and discretion it is wont to inspect and admire, — than the spirit and habits of such a Christian are moulded after the pattern of his Lord and Friend. He is familiar with the meekness of Christ, and has an eye to appreciate its beauty; and it begets meekness in himself. He perceives distinctly the gentleness of Christ, and has a heart to feel its excellence; and it begets gentleness of spirit, of conversation, of conduct. He studies the tender kindness of Christ toward the poor, and the sick, and the widow, and the mourner, and has a heart to feel its loveliness; and it opens *his* heart, and *his* hand, and *his* words of comfort, to the sons and daughters of sorrow. He discovers more and more of his Saviour's love as it is betokened in his suffering of death, — in the works of his hand, — in the bounties of his providence, — in his promises, — in his consolations, — in his sympathy, — in his fellowship; and his heart is impelled to new and stronger emotions of Faith. He lifts up his eye and reads the proofs of Christ's sufficiency as High-Priest, and as Bishop, and as Advocate, and as Shepherd; he lifts up his eye and beholds the Supremacy of Christ, "far above all principality and power and might and dominion and every name that is named"; and *again* his heart is impelled to Faith, — yes, and to Hope, and to Courage, and to Patience, and to Love, and to Obedience.

In like manner the knowledge of Christ operates to the culture of every branch of Christian virtue; toward man and God; toward holiness and sin; toward the good and the wicked;—of thought, of feeling, of devotion, of word, of business, of charity.

But enough of illustration. Hear one word of testimony. "His divine power," says an inspired Christian, "hath given unto us *all things* that pertain unto *life* and *godliness*." How? By what means? "*Through the knowledge of him* that hath called us to glory and virtue." And again, "We all, with open face, beholding as in a glass *the glory of the Lord*, are changed *into the same image* from glory to glory."

And thus, by *the knowledge of Christ*, the Christian grows; grows in his Master's likeness; grows in his Master's glory and beauty; grows in *every* grace; grows in the form and symmetry and *power* of godliness. It is so in heaven, my brother. It is to be so when Christ shall appear in his glory. "We shall be like him, for we shall *see* him *as he is*." And if it be so in heaven, must it not be so on earth? If his saints are wrought more and more into his likeness by the knowledge of him *there*, will they not be wrought into his likeness by means of the knowledge of him *here?*

But, O brother! if what I say, and if what the Scripture says, upon this point, fail to waken within you a lively conviction of its truth, go to some disciple who has been taught by long experience; to some one who is versed in the mystery of godliness; to some one who bears about the tokens of a rich and fruitful piety; and ask him where his heart has burned most with Faith and Love and Hope and every other Christian affection. Ask him where the evil inclinations of his heart have been most subdued. Ask him where he has been most impelled to holiness of outward life. He will say, at the foot of the cross; in the closet; where he has seen the most of Christ; where he has heard the most of him; where he has felt the most of him; where he has grown the most in the knowledge of him. Yes; and he would say too, "Live *thou also* under the light of his glory; grow *thou* in the *knowledge* of Christ, if thou wouldst grow in grace."

But there is another result of the knowledge of Christ. While it pushes the Christian graces, of heart and life, toward perfection, it has set in motion graces which, in their turn, bear fruit also. "If these things be in you and abound, they make you that ye shall be neither *barren* nor *unfruitful* in the knowledge of our Lord Jesus Christ."

Set Christian affections to work, and you have set the Christian to work. If he has slept before, he sleeps no longer. If he has been a loiterer and an eyesore in the vineyard of his Lord, he is so no longer. *No* Christian can keep alive a *heartfelt* knowledge of Christ, *no* Christian can be sensible of the excellence and glory of Christ, without imbibing the spirit and the *habits* of his Master. "The love of Christ *constraineth* us." It impels us. When we perceive what *he is*, and feel it; when thus we are infused with the *life* of piety; we take up forthwith *the business* of piety. We go about doing good. We employ our talents in the service of our Lord. They are no longer in a napkin, — out of sight, — out of use. We are on our feet. We are at our posts. We cannot help it. The knowledge of Christ constrains us, — impels us, — "bears us away like a strong and resistless torrent."* We are bringing something to pass, — in the family, — in the church, — in the street; something for Christ; something for him who loved us; something for him who

* Doddridge's Expositor, on 2 Cor. v. 14, and on Phil. i. 23, note.

hath called us, and baptized us, and communed with us, and comforted us. We are doing it by prayer, interceding for our households. We are doing it by instruction, teaching our households. We are doing it in our intercourse with our brethren; by exhortation; by counsel; by sympathy; by encouragement; by prayer.

O, who *can* be a neuter, — a drone, — a grovelling gatherer of the muck and straw and tinsel of this world, — or a puling craver for the mere nosegays or philosophy of religion, — when the knowledge of Christ is lively within him; when Christ dwelleth in his heart; when Christ is formed in him the hope of glory?

But the enlivening of Christian graces by the knowledge of Christ brings yet another result. Not only does the tree produce fruit, but the fruit produces seed, and the seed produces fruit again. The knowledge of Christ rouses piety; and piety impels to consistency; and consistency goes abroad, with her robes of modesty and her voice of eloquence, like an angel, among the scoffers and the hard-hearted. Yes, like an angel, she can win *her* way to many a haunt of vice, to many a hovel of jealous and ignorant poverty, where a Pharisee, with his phylacteries and his tithes and his long prayers and his widow's spoils, would not go if he could, and could not go if he dared. Yes, like an angel, *she* can win her way to ears that are deaf as adders' to others; *she*, by the blessing of God, can still tongues which spit derision like serpents at others; and *charm* them, too; and teach them to *extol* religion. *She*, by God's blessing, can speak of Christ's love, and touch the *heart* of the stupid and worldly-minded, when a halting, fitful, inconsistent disciple will leave no blessing behind him in the day of his death; but his "remembrance shall perish," and his "name shall rot."

O for a piety which shall *disperse* itself! O for a piety, — a noiseless, gentle, unpretending piety, — which men may recognize as my gift from heaven; which shall leave the softening impress of its influence upon other hearts, and be whispered by other tongues when this heart and this tongue are awaiting the resurrection! O, then, for the knowledge of my Redeemer! O for a clear and growing and impelling discovery of the glory of Him who died upon the cross!

But, brother beloved, follow me a step farther, for my heart is in this matter. Look at the influence of the knowledge of Christ upon the Christian's happiness.

There is such a thing as peace of mind. There is such a thing as sweet peace, — " perfect peace." Yes, — here in this vale of tears, — here, amid all the distractions and changes and responsibilities of a wicked world. There is such a thing as a mind " quiet from the fear of evil." There is such a thing as eying the rising cloud of a temporal affliction, as looking upon the cup of bitterness which Providence is mingling, and yet saying with a peaceful, blissful spirit, " Thy will be done ! " There is such a thing as baring ourselves to the rod without a fear of one stripe more than is needful, or of one stroke which shall cut too deep. Nay, more. There is such a thing as sweet and perfect peace, even under the testimony of the Law. We *can* be conscious of our past sins ; we *can* perceive much of their enormity ; we *can* be conscious of present imperfection ; we *can* be vividly aware of the terrors of the second death, and of our own personal inability to escape it ; we *can* lie down to die, and bid adieu to husband, wife, children, to all that are bound to our hearts here ; we *can* step down into the river which alone separates us from the solemnities and decisions of eternity and yet be at peace.*

And there is such a thing as being comforted when we mourn. There is such a thing as having a wounded heart healed, — a throbbing heart soothed, — an aching heart consoled. There is such a thing as getting "the oil of joy for mourning; the garment of praise for the spirit of heaviness"; — a different thing, very, from healing the hurt, slightly, with amusement, or business, or philosophy so called. There is such a thing as affliction itself being turned into blessing; mourning itself into rejoicing; lamentations themselves into praises. The very death and burial of an earthly hope — an occasion to-day of the bitterest grief — may be to-morrow a source of the purest blessing. The very time and place

* When Bishop Butler lay on his death-bed, he called for his chaplain, and said, "Though I have endeavored to avoid sin and to please God to the utmost of my power, yet, from the consciousness of perpetual infirmities, I am still afraid to die." "My lord," said the chaplain, "you have forgotten that Jesus Christ is a Saviour." "True," was the answer, "but how shall I know that he is a Saviour for me?" "My lord, it is written, 'He that cometh to me I will in no wise cast out.'" "True," said the Bishop, "and I am surprised, that, though I have read that Scripture a thousand times over, I never felt its virtue till this moment. And now I die happy." — *N. Y. Observer*, *May*, 1840.

of its death may be the birthplace and the birthday of a better. The tomb where we bury it may be the very spot of resurrection for another and a better. From its very ashes there may spring to life a new one,—a better one,—yea, one "full of immortality."

These things are very precious blessings. Neither their reality nor their value can be questioned. Both have been proved by the actual experience of thousands. But how do they spring into life? How do they become the portion of men? Whence flows this peace in view of evils temporal and of evils spiritual? Whence this comfort under the most severe tribulations of life?

I answer,—through *the knowledge of Christ.* Yes; let the Christian but open his eye and his heart to the character of his Saviour; let him but perceive and *feel* the truth that *Jesus* governs; *then* he can foresee the coming tempest; *then* he can watch the mingling of his cup; *then* he can look at the uplifted rod;—*sure* that he needs them; *sure* that they will be meted to him in tenderness. *Then* he can trust, and trust, and be at peace.

Let him but perceive and *feel* Christ's sufficiency as his Sacrifice; his fidelity and ability and love as his Shepherd; his power as his Advocate; and what though he has sinned? what if the Law do thunder? what if the adversary do roar? what if temptations and tempters do beset him? what if there are unslain corruptions within him? what if he be helpless? There is blood enough for his sprinkling; grace enough for his pardon; power enough for his purging; and Love enough for his surety. *Then*—he can rest himself in peace. He can quietly, yet humbly and obediently, *leave* himself, for acquittal and salvation, with the faithful Shepherd of Israel.

Let him but know the sympathy and fellowship of Christ; let him but know them by having tested them in the way of confidential communion; and *then*, when the cloud of grief bursts, when bereavement strips him, when some creature staff fails him, he will find his way, like the pelted bird, to his place of refuge, like the hunted hart to his covert. He will throw himself upon Christ as a bosom Friend. He will show him his wounds. He will tell him his grief. And He who has stricken will heal. Thus life will come to him from death; hope from darkness. Trouble impels him to his Saviour; and there, upon *his* bosom, receiving *his* consolations, he gains a peculiar and precious foretaste of heaven, and an earnest of salvation.

> "The men of grace have found
> Glory begun below.
> Celestial fruits, on earthly ground,
> From Faith and Hope, may grow."

But do you ask yet again, Whence flows this peace? and whence this comfort? Then I answer again,—not in my own words,—"*Acquaint* now thyself with him and be at peace; thereby good shall come unto thee." "Grace and peace [shall] be multiplied unto you through the *knowledge* of God and of Jesus Christ our Lord."

Now, then, can either you or I compute the value of this knowledge of Christ? Can either you or I compute the excellency of its fruits? Well,—well might Paul exclaim, "I count all things *loss* for the excellency of the knowledge of Christ Jesus my Lord." And well may we echo his exclamation. Well may we plead continually with this prayer upon our lips,—"Lord, Lord, evermore give us this bread."

Is there any equivalent for this knowledge? Is there any thing else which will "yield us the *peaceable* fruits of righteousness"? any thing else which will train us up to the fulness of the stature of perfection in Christ? any thing else which will invigorate hope, faith, love, obedience, meekness, brotherly kindness, charity, every other virtue? any thing else which will impel us to fidelity, to steadfastness, to labor, to self-denial, to consistency? any thing else which can fill us with peace? which can open to us the fountain of God's consolation in our days of trial? What?

As for the world, — the things of the world, and the friendship of the world, — they are powerless. They are not to be reckoned. They have no more intrinsic fitness to the soul's wants, than the doctrines of the Bible have to the body's wants. But go to the Bible. What else is there even *there* which can do these things for us? "The *Law* is weak through the flesh." "The *Law* is our schoolmaster" only "to *bring us to Christ.*" Look, then, at the Gospel. But what is there *there* which can thus serve us? Why! *Christ* is the Alpha and the Omega of the Gospel. All the *Gospel's* doctrines are both senseless and powerless save as they *teach us Christ.*

O, it is in vain to hope for growth in grace, for sanctification of heart, for holiness of life, for the influence of consistent example, for peace, for comfort, for any thing by which we may adorn the doctrine of our Lord, do good, overcome the world, and ripen for heaven, — without the knowledge of Christ! *This* is the great secret of piety. *This* is the secret of its growth. *This* is the great antidote to sin; to spiritual slumber; to stupidity; to the seductions of the world; to an unquiet mind; to a bleeding heart. It is *this*, brother. Nothing else, whether in heaven above or the earth beneath.

Do you say, "There is the Holy Spirit; *He* is to sanctify; *He* is to guide; *He* is to comfort; I wait for Him to come and revive me"? Show me — show me — a single evidence that the Holy Spirit ever sanctifies, ever revives, ever makes useful or happy, save through the truth, — the *knowledge* of the truth, — the knowledge of the "truth *as it is in Jesus*," — and your reference to the Spirit will hold good. But, my brother, *not till* then.

No; no. Were you as well taught as Paul in the doctrine of election, or in the doctrine of regeneration, or in the doctrine of the Holy Spirit's agency, or in the nature and necessity of personal holiness, or in the terrors of a broken Law, — the blessings which I have specified cannot accrue to you in their fulness, and some of them not at all, unless you maintain an intimate, endearing knowledge of Christ. They cannot be yours unless, like Paul, you make all these doctrines your conductors to the cross, your interpreters of Jesus.

How easy it is, now, to discern the great and lamentable cause of the deficiencies of Christian experience, — *ignorance of Jesus Christ.* It is this — which makes Christians tire in their course. It is this — which clogs their feet. It is this — which makes them reel and fall and go to sleep. It makes them heavy-hearted, and unsteady, and faint, and fearful, and desponding, and worldly-minded. It betrays them into by-paths. It clouds their hopes. It silences their songs. It unbalances their graces. It unnerves their arms. It makes them false witnesses of the grace of God. It withers all those beauties and blessings which the knowledge of Christ imparts. It is not the world that does all this. It is not the adversary. No. It is ignorance of Christ. Were *he* in lively remembrance in their hearts daily; if they did but keep *his* excellence imaged upon the mirror of their affections; think you they would be entrapped by a paltry world? think you they would not resist the Devil? think you they would not keep chains and fetters upon indwelling sin? think you they would go mourning all the day?

I have known two aged Christians. They had passed their threescore years and ten, and most of that time they had worn the badge of Christ. Of their Christian histories I cannot testify, but in one particular. One has fallen asleep in Jesus. The other still lingers here, — I doubt not because she must yet learn more of Christ ere she will be meet for heaven. She who died, stood for a long time upon the brink of Jordan; expecting the coming of her ministering angels. She seemed to understand well those words, — "O death! where is thy sting? O grave! where is thy victory?" And what gave her courage and peace? What strengthened her so long under the very shadow of dissolution? It was her knowledge of Christ. Her eye and heart were filled with him. Her tongue could speak *his* name, and talk of *his* love, and utter *his* promises, and mention *his* cross. That — was the secret of her serenity. It solved the mystery of her peaceful departure.

The other has been starved, her whole life, upon polemic divinity. She has hung upon the skirts of every battle which has been fought between religious partisans for half a century. She has been filled with "free agency," and "decrees," and "Trinity," and "baptism," and "terms of communion"; while scarce a crumb has fallen to her from the table of Christ; scarce a ray has she caught from his glory. And now there she stands upon the brink of the river, shivering and fearing to depart, — because she sees not and feels not the presence and fulness of Christ.

Brother in Christ, the bones of many such a disciple are mementos of the sad results of ignorance of Christ. They are bleaching beacons for your warning. Had they tongues, every one of them would cry out to confirm the truth which I have tried to illustrate.

Nay more, my brother. The names of many of your own generation have been hung up before you on the scroll of infamy. The ministers at the altar have fallen. And the warning has been rung in your ears and mine, from amid the noise and consternation of their apostasy, — "Count all things loss, — count all things *loss*, — for the excellency of the knowledge of Christ Jesus your Lord."

Progression is as much a law of spiritual as of animal life. The oak does not burst with a sudden explosion from the acorn. The flower does not expand itself forthwith from the parent seed. The lark does not burst from its shell, and fly up toward heaven all fledged and strong, piping its clear melody, *at once*, to God. The man does not leap up from his swaddling-clothes, passing with one convulsive stride from weak and whining infancy to the full glory of bearded and muscular maturity. Neither does the child of God leap up at once to the fulness of the stature of perfection in Christ Jesus. *He* also is first a babe; then, a child; then, step by step, a full-grown man. It is so with Christian knowledge. It is so with the knowledge of Christ. It would be more rational to suppose that the mind of a young pupil could at once stride from the multiplication-table to all the mysteries and involutions of the higher mathematics, than to suppose that he whose spiritual eye is but just opened can comprehend at a glance all the glory of Him who hath "set down with the Father on his throne"; before whom angels bow and seraphs cover their faces.

"The bridegroom rejoiceth over the bride." He has much to tell you about the pearl which he has found and won. He thinks — poor man — that he knows the worth of his treasure *now*. But go to him when the cares and the checkered alternations of life have furrowed his cheek and bared his brow and bleached his locks. Go to him when he has *tested* the wife of his youth through joys and through troubles; when he has drunk deep at the fountain of her sympathy, and seen her constancy unharmed in many a furnace;—and he will laugh at the simplicity and boasting and praises of his bridal days. He will tell you, that he knew not whereof he affirmed in the times of his first exultation. He will tell you, that,—though time has worn out youth, and cares have faded beauty,—yet time and cares both have brought to light many a *better* grace, and bound many a dearer cord of union about him and the wife of his bosom.

So it is with the Christian in his discovery of the fulness of Christ. In the day of his espousal he *thinks* that he knows his treasure. Something of it he does know. Something of it he does feel. It is indeed *Christ* upon whom he leans. It is indeed *his* voice that he hears. It is indeed of *his* beauty and loveliness that he is enamored. I say,—he *thinks* that he knows his Saviour. But, O, how little he knows! Go to him when years of fellowship and sympathy have taught him wisdom; when he has tested the constancy of Christ through many a sea of trouble; when he has sat at the feet of Christ and studied his glory through many a storm. Go to him when he has almost passed over the journey of his pilgrimage; and he will smile at the remembrance of his spiritual infancy,—not because his knowledge of Christ was then untrue or insipid, but because he *thought*, in his unfledged youth, that he understood the excellence of Christ. True, in his spiritual childhood the knowledge of Christ was reviving and clear. Yet he will speak of it now as only the knowledge of his spiritual alphabet; as the A B C of his Christian wisdom.

The love of a young disciple is like a stream at its fountain-head. True, it goes down the mountain-side by leaps. It laughs, and sparkles, and babbles in the sunshine, like a thing of perfect life and gladness. But it has not half the depth, nor breadth, nor speed, nor power, as when it has reached the valley; as when it has taken tributary waters to its bosom; as when it flows noiselessly along, clothing a thousand meadows and hamlets with verdure and fatness. So, I say, is the love of a Christian for Christ; buoyant and sprightly in its youth, but mighty and large and rich its manhood. And the *secret* of its increase is this,—that in its youth the *knowledge* of Christ was comparatively small; in manhood, that knowledge has multiplied a thousand-fold.

It being true, then, that love to Christ is progressive, and that the *knowledge* of Christ (which is the aliment of that love) is progressive also, it is an interesting point of inquiry, by what means this knowledge may be increased.

Evidently it must be by means of *effort.* We must *take pains* to grow in the knowledge of Christ, as well as to grow in any other knowledge. Mere wishing and sighing for it will not bring it. Mere mourning over our ignorance will not bring it. Why is it, that the schoolboy, with all his drilling, is sometimes a bungling stammerer over his book? Does he not *wish* to read? to read with ease? to read with accuracy? Certainly he does. But he hates *the cost.* He wants a royal road to knowledge. He wants to dodge the toil. *Of course*, he is a bungler. Why is it that the man of strong health and strong sinews is poor; his wife in rags, his children hungry? Does he not *wish* to have the means of livelihood? Does he not *wish* for wealth? Does he not mourn over his poverty? Does he not sincerely sigh for a better lot? Most certainly he does. But he hates the cost, the toil of wealth. He loves to turn himself in his bed and cry, "A little more sleep,—a little more sleep." He loves to lounge at the corners of the streets. *Of course*, he is poor. Of course, —although he has health and strength. Of course,—although both neighbor and nature would pay as good bounty for his labor as for that of others.

It is a law which God has established, that blessings shall come by price. He who would eat must work. He who would be rich must work. He who would be well versed in natural science must study. And so, he who would be proficient in religious knowledge—in the knowledge of Christ—must labor for it. The alternative is before him; either be indolent and take the consequences of an unhappy and shameful ignorance, or be diligent in the study of Christ and reap the blessed rewards of his knowledge. There is no other course. *Wishing* for piety, and enjoyment, and consistency, and peace, will never bring them. *Wishing* for a familiar knowledge of the fulness and grace of Christ will never bring *it*, nor those its blissful fruits. Never Never. Mourning over your religious ignorance, my brother, and over the bitter consequences of that ignorance,—I grant it may be sincere and hearty,—but it will never mend matters with you. Ten thousand sluggish tears, and sighs, and groans, will never draw down upon you one beam of light,—one smile,—one sweet manifestation,—from the face of Jesus Christ. Never. Never.

There *are* schools where you may be taught of Christ. There *are* "instructors in Christ." Do you ever take pains to watch the events of providence? Do you ever piously, seriously, earnestly, count over the blessings of your life, and its afflictions? Do you ever notice obstacles which sometimes spring up to keep you from sin and temptation? Do you ever *dwell* upon the truth that the hand of your Redeemer is in all these things? and his loving-kindness? and his grace? Do you ever sit down to look at them, and admire them, and enjoy them, as fruits of his sufferings, as the purchases of his blood? Do you ever thus hear and regard *their* sweet testimony of Jesus? If you do not, no wonder if you are ignorant of Christ as *they* declare him; no wonder if you do not find daily teachers of his grace in the events of your life; no wonder if you do not *grow* in the knowledge of Christ. You ought to sit and hearken to the whisperings of his Providence; to the music of his works and deeds. *This* you ought to do, if you would learn Him who loved you and died for you. *This* you ought to do if you would reap the precious fruits which grow upon the tree of the knowledge of Christ.

Do you ever take pains to study the testimony of Scripture concerning Christ? I do not ask you if you read your Bible. Do you *search* it? eagerly? prayerfully? habitually? Do you search out Christ in it? O, how fully the Scriptures testify of Him! Precious words there about his love; about his value; about his power; about his blood! Every doctrine speaks of him; every prophecy; every type and shadow; every historical fact, from the creation to the destruction of the holy city. There are a thousand tongues there which make melody in praise of Jesus. Brother, are you wont to go and hear their music? Are you wont to go and hear until your heart is touched and fired, and your own tongue impelled to join the chorus? If not, I do not wonder if you are ignorant of Christ. I do not wonder if you are barren and unfruit ful and joyless. It must be so. It must be so.

Do you love the sanctuary? Do you love the assemblies of his saints? Do you love to go *wherever* Christ's name is uttered and his goodness explained? *Do you go?* Do you *hear?* Do you watch and strive there to *learn* something of Christ? Brother, it hath pleased God to give efficacy to preaching, yea, to "the *foolishness* of preaching." It hath pleased Christ to manifest himself in the assemblies of his saints; even where but two or three are gathered together in his name. And if you lightly esteem, and needlessly slight *these* means of grace, I do not wonder at your ignorance, and your barrenness, your feeble faith, your half-expiring love. A coal of fire will *go out* if alone. It will burn brighter and brighter with others. And your joy and light and fervor will go out without the aliment of Christian fellowship. Do you say that you lightly esteem these means of grace because you have but little spirituality? Nay, nay, the other way. You have little spirituality because you lightly esteem these means of grace; because you do not prize them and use them as teachers of Jesus.

Do you, or do you not, keep Christ's words?

One of his disciples once said to him, when on earth, "Lord, how is it that thou wilt manifest thyself unto us, and not unto the world? Jesus answered and said unto him, If a man love me, he will keep my words,"—and Christ's words concern the sanctuary, the Scriptures, the government of his hands, and our daily life in *all* things;—"he will keep my words, and my Father will love him, and we will come unto him, and *make our abode with* him."

And how is it with your closet? *There* Jesus manifests himself peculiarly. It is in the hour of secret appeal, when the business and friends of the world are excluded, in the hour when we cast ourselves upon his love, when we lay the secrets of our hearts before him with *affectionate* and *trustful ingenuousness*, that Christ most preciously manifests and communicates himself. Not by visible presence, not by audible voice, but by awaking us to new and fresh perceptions of himself, by bringing into conscious and vigorous vibration those cords of endearment which subsist between himself and us; as verily and as effectually as if by vision or by speech. The actual sympathy, the active communion, between Christ and his beloved here *in no wise* depend upon organs of sense. The *spirit* of Christ, and the *spirit* of his closet-worshipper, are as free of sense as though the one had no glorified body, and the other no fleshly. The hour of their exclusive spiritual intercourse is one of spiritual and real interchange. The disciple expounds himself to Christ, and Christ to the disciple. The weak goes thence strengthened; the timid, emboldened; the wavering, believing; the afflicted, consoled; the desolate, *conscious* of a Friend; — each acquisition being the result of new and timely perceptions of Christ, and each perception the result of his direct manifestation. Such has ever been Christian *experience;* and such ever *will be.* There must *you* go; thus must *you* deport yourself, if you would grow in the knowledge of your Saviour; if you would gather the most richly of "the true bread from heaven." Do YOU?

Do you ever, or never, give up business or diversion or ease for the sake of going to the closet, to the sanctuary, to the more private fellowship of Christ's people; for the sake of using any and every means which can increase your knowledge of your Redeemer? How is it? If you do not, is Christ to *you* "the chiefest among ten thousand," the one "altogether lovely"? And if he is not, are you *his?* And if you are not his, are you safe? Is your hope good? Will it anchor you in the day of your dissolution?

By your obligations to glorify the Lord,— by the brevity and value of your life,—I beseech you to know Christ more, and more, and more. Study him. Use the means—*all* the means—of searching his "unsearchable riches." Otherwise you will not be a growing, happy Christian; you will not meet your obligations to Christ, your precious Saviour. If the knowledge of Christ is the charm of heaven, it is the charm of the Christian on earth. If this is the secret of the Church's holiness, of its harmony, of its fellowship there, it is the secret of its holiness, and happiness, and fellowship here. "Grace and peace" must "be multiplied unto you through *the knowledge* of God and of Jesus our Lord."

I am aware that I have given but an outline of this subject. I am aware that I have not fully done even this. I am aware that I have not noticed the fundamental truth, that this knowledge of Christ is itself the *constituent element* of eternal life; that I have not attempted to illustrate the declaration of our

Saviour, "This is Life eternal, that they might *know* thee the only true God, and Jesus Christ whom thou hast sent"; neither that significant word of the prophet, "By his *knowledge* shall my righteous servant justify many." What I have said is but suggestive, and feebly suggestive. But will you, my Christian brother, seize upon whatever of truth I have sketched, and use it as a stimulant to your own heart? As you lay aside this little volume, will you retain in your memory, and cherish for prayerful meditation, "the knowledge of Christ" in all its phases and bearings? If you will, I shall have been his instrument for your profit, to your joy, to your usefulness, to your greater measure of spiritual Life. If you will, my object is attained. To nothing higher do I herein aspire. I point you to Christ. I commend him to you. I commend you to him. I leave you at his feet, for his fellowship. I would also "bow my knees unto the Father of our Lord Jesus Christ, of whom the whole family in heaven and earth is named, that he would grant you according to the riches of his glory, to be strengthened with might by his Spirit in the inner man, that Christ may dwell in your heart by faith; that, being rooted and grounded in love, you may be able to comprehend, with all saints, what is the breadth, and length, and depth, and height; and to know the love of Christ, which passeth knowledge, that you may be filled with all the fulness of God."

IX.

THE WEALTH OF THE BELIEVER.

Did I wish to laugh to scorn the creed of Christians, I would not point to the doctrines of miracles and everlasting perdition. I would not point to the twofold nature of Christ, as metaphysically absurd; nor to the unmixed humanity of Christ, as involving the Scriptures in self-contradiction; nor to vicarious atonement, as grossly inconsistent with Divine justice; nor to the sufferings, *without* atonement, of one who knew no sin, as *doubly* inconsistent with justice. I would simply point to these words of Paul, addressed to his contemporaries at Corinth, " *All* things are *yours.*"

Compare this with other assertions of the Bible. Where any thing else so startling, so staggering to faith? Not only the Son given as a sacrifice for the guilty, as a Redeemer of the lost, but "all things" else beside! Not only the greatest, but the greatest and the least! Not only the choicest gem in the coffer, not the priceless, peerless treasure only, but the coffer itself and all its stores! Not only bounty without similitude, but bounty without measure and without end!

And yet as Christians we would point to these same words with exultation. We would point to this wondrous heirship and say, "Here is brilliance which seems like *heaven's;* here is bounty which looks like *God's.* If you would know what He is in whom we trust; if you would know the boundless grace in which we rejoice; if you would know the portion which we choose; man of doubts, of little faith, look *here.* Look at this charter of our inheritance, and tell us who is a God like unto our God."

Yes; it needs a towering faith to receive this assurance as a very truth. It needs an eye which can bear a dazzling glory, to survey it. But when received and when surveyed, it becomes a precious and peculiar tie between the soul and God. It is so great that it is hardly to be believed; and yet because it is so great, it is beyond value to the believer. It is so vast and so full of splendor, that it may confound the sceptic. But the Christian sees in its very brightness and vastness the impress, the seal, the signature of God; and holds it, and believes it, and glories in it, because it is so full of God-like richness and God-like grace.

"They are not all Israel which are of Israel; neither because they are the seed of Abraham are they all children." "He is not a Jew who is one outwardly; neither is that circumcision which is outward in the flesh; but he is a Jew who is one inwardly, and circumcision is that of the heart, in the spirit and not in the letter." So they are not all Christ's who are of Christ. Many adopt his name; many wear his badge; many speak his language, — who are not his. Who, then, *are* his? Who *belong* to him? Who are *his* people? What is it to be Christ's?

Suppose we adopt the sinful habits of the world, and its sickening and soulless frivolities. We pitch our tents beside its fountains of impure pleasure. We leap amid its eddies of delirious and noisy mirth. We put the cup to our neighbor's lips and wring out to the wife of his youth its dregs of wormwood and gall. Is this being *Christ's?* Why! Jesus Christ says, "Follow me." Is *this* treading where he has trodden? Are the prints of his footsteps — *here?* Where? And if we do not "follow" Christ, are we his?

But suppose less. We are habitually neglectful of spiritual duties. We are not wont to praise and honor God before men. We have no dear communion with him. We have no altar where we burn the sweet incense of secret devotion. Is *this* being Christ's? Is *this* following his steps? — his steps who shaped his life and bore his cross for the honor of his Father? And if we do not "follow" him, are we Christ's?

But suppose still less. We are habitually neglectful of moral duties. We give no oil and no wine and no place of rest to him who has been wounded by thieves. We have no ministrations for the sick; no bounty for the poor; no *good* sympathy for the afflicted and bereaved. We are rough, or uncourteous, or repulsive in our ordinary transactions. We are harsh, or selfish, or sullen, at our homes. We ruffle the temper, we disturb the peace, of friends, of children, of parents, or we thwart their plans for enjoyment or duty. I ask, Is *this* treading in the steps of Christ? I ask, Is *this* "following" him? Is *this* being his? No. No. "If we have not the *spirit* of Christ, we are none of his." We cannot serve two masters. We cannot serve God and Mammon. We cannot be Belial's and Christ's. If we are the world's in our habits; if we are the world's in despising the honor and fellowship of God; if we are the world's in our dispositions, then we are not Christ's. We may be, we are, we must be, his, just as "every beast of the forest is his, and the cattle upon a thousand hills"; but we are not his chosen ones, — his beloved, — his espoused.

What, then, is it to be Christ's? It is this. To live for him. To be his property in the best sense; his *devoted* ones. To be his by oath, by covenant, by service. To "present ourselves a living sacrifice," — body, — soul, — all, — to Christ. To write his name upon every power and upon every member. To bring the outward life and the inward spirit to his baptism. To open the eye and the heart to the touching testimonials of his love, to the exciting beauties of his face, to the enlivening glories of his Divine grace; till the outbursting tribute of the soul shall be, "Here, Lord, I give myself away." It is to have toward Christ such a spirit that "none of us liveth to himself, and no man dieth to himself"; that "whether we live, we live unto the Lord, and whether we die, we die unto the Lord"; that "whether we live, therefore, or die" hereby, — herein, — "we are the *Lord's*."

Who, then, are devoted to Christ? Who have the spirit of entire consecration to their Lord? Who are striving to mould their outward deeds, their speech, their habits, their inward dispositions, after the pattern of Christ? Whoever they are, — although their steps are feeble, — although their garments are not yet purged to perfect whiteness, — although you may detect many a blemish in their deportment, — yet, having this spirit of devotedness to Christ, they are hereby *his*. Yes; and if Christ's, then "joint heirs with Christ." If Christ's, then heirs with him who is "heir of all things." These are they to whom all wealth is given. These are they to whom all things are wealth. So says the inspired writer, "All things are yours; whether Paul, or Apollos, or Cephas, or the world, or life, or death, or things present, or things to come, — all are yours." And who are *they?* "And ye are *Christ's*."

But are all things *property* to those who are Christ's? — the ministry, with its blemishes, its strifes, and its defections? as well as the ministry with its graces, its eloquence, and its piety? Are *all* things their property? Have they wealth in all things, even in the world with its scorn and its hatred? in life with its wants, its unceasing fluctuations, and its plagues? in death with its unreported terrors? in things present, in gold, in silver, in luxury, in the unceasing tide of events which is rolling on from year to year? in things to come,—in the dreadful doom of judgment as well as in its acquittal? in hell as well as in heaven?

Yes; property in all. Yes, every thing that now is, is tributary to their profit; and every thing that is to come, shall be. Every thing —willing or unwilling, high or low, good or bad—is moved and removed, and lives and grows and acts and ceases, for their highest and purest bliss. Every thing is theirs and is laboring for their good; and every thing, without exception, shall; and none can hinder it. Yes; in the very ragings of a troubled world; in the most fearful shapes of depravity you can name; in the noisy surgings of the lake of woe; they have ministering servants,—*property*,—more, better, richer, surer property, ye men of earthly pleasures and earthly riches, than *ye* have in your mirth and laughter, in your merchandise and gold.

All things are theirs; not in their *possession*, but in their *service;* not controlled *by* them, but controlled *for* them. Paul and Apollos, and Cephas and Judas; the whole line of the ministry, good and bad, true and false; sincere men and hypocrites; saints and castaways; have not touched a single spring of influence, — have not set in motion a single train of events, — without bringing blessings upon those who are Christ's. All things are in the hand of their Lord. "Unto the Son, all things are delivered of the Father." And he shall overrule all and overturn all, so that, in every event and by every agent, the purposes of God shall be accomplished, and the glory of God — without a shade, without a veil, without a cloud — shall be revealed.

What are the chief desires of those who are Christ's? Those which were, and ever will be, his, — "that the Father may be glorified in the Son"; that "they may behold his glory"; that they may be purged clean without spot or blemish. And he who overrules and overturns, — he who holds the winds and the seas and thoughts and hearts and all things, — shall guide and govern all for the accomplishment of these objects.

Thus every influence of the ministry; and every wave, and burden, and bubble upon the tide of time; every object; every form of sin, and every trophy of grace; every day of sunshine, and every night of storm; every ministration of affliction, and every one of prosperity, — shall all serve for the full development of our Redeemer's glory, and for the preparation of his people for his courts. The men of the world are thus overruled and overturned. Their schemes, their wisdom, their enterprise, their opposition to the truth, their silver and their gold, their rise and their fall, their birth and their death, and their perdition, — are all but make-weights in the balances of God's purposes. In each, and in the use of each, and in the remotest influence of each, is a preparation-work for the coming of his kingdom; a purifying work upon the hearts of his people; and a key to the unsearchable riches of his excellence. They are "hewers of wood and drawers of water for the house of the Lord." They polish and arrange the members of his spiritual temple, — unwittingly, unwillingly; but verily and perfectly. And even in the death of the body and the death of the soul, they unveil the brilliant mystery both of Grace and of Justice.

So, too, are the life and the death of the Christian himself overturned and overruled. Every particular of comfort and of trial, of conflict and deliverance, of hope and darkness, of poverty and abundance; every buffeting of Satan; every thorn in the flesh; the time, the place, the particulars of his dissolution; all are made tributary to the same ends, — the perfection of the soul, the spread of the Gospel, and the display of God's glory.

So, too, with things present. The rise and fall of empires; the strifes and cruelties of men; every thing which transpires from the rising to the setting sun; each is made to give in its contribution to the same great ends.

And so with things to come. In the destruction of the world; in the resurrection of the dead; in the decisions of the judgment; in the bliss of heaven, and in the hopeless woe of hell; in pardon and in condemnation; in each shall be a fresh and distinct and peculiar development of the boundless glory of God. In each, and by each, shall "the Father be glorified in the Son."

See now the bearing of these things upon those who are Christ's. See how all things are theirs. See how all things are bringing tributary offerings to their feet. See how all things, and all events, and all men, and all eternity, are their ministering servants. Every thing is fulfilling the desires of their hearts. Every thing is working for that which is their pleasure. Every one is giving impulse to the operations of grace. Every one hereafter shall reveal the story of its influence. Every story shall reveal Redeeming Love. Every new disclosure of Redeeming Love shall give new rapture to the admiring, adoring saint. Thus every thing is ministering to his blessedness. Every thing is culturing the vintage which he shall pluck in heaven. Every thing is making ready the cluster and the cup for his banquet in the Father's kingdom. Every thing is preparing him for his inheritance; and his inheritance for him.

O ye men of worldly hopes! do you despise the Christian? Do you look upon his lot as pitiful, because he is a man of secret burdens and many imperfections? because he denies himself where you give the rein to indulgence? because he passes by the fountains of pleasure at which you drink to fulness and satiety? Look at his boundless, endless heritage. Look at the inventory of his limitless possessions. Look! it covers all things. It covers *you* — and *yours.* Are you rich? Your silver and your gold are — his. Are you free, and do you boast of liberty? Your bodies are — his. Your souls are — his. Your very members and thoughts, your hearts, your passions, the noontide of your lives, the heyday of your prosperity, the gathering twilight of your declining sun, the coming darkness of your starless midnight, all — all — are his. In each there is, or is to be, some disclosure of those depths of Grace or Justice which are the sea of his enjoyments, the light and the life of his heaven. You are bringing sheaves into his storehouse. You are paying tribute-money into his treasury. Your very pride, your scorn, your jest, your cutting accusations of inconsistency, are the smelting-furnace of his spirit. They are the fire and the fuel with which his Purifier is purging out his dross to bring him to the brilliant splendor and the beauteous pureness of the virgin silver. It is not His will that any one of all such shall perish. They are in his keeping in the midst of their troubles. It is his will, that *all* things shall be theirs; you, — yours, — your life, with its every word, and deed, and influence; your death with its every terror; and your eternity, — if ye go there, what ye now are, the servants of the world, — your eternity, with its every woe.

Such is the wealth of those who are Christ's. It is wealth beyond computation, — without limit and without exhaustion. It is theirs by covenant; theirs by oath; theirs to-day; and theirs for ever. It is theirs, for they are Christ's It is theirs, for they are the fruits of his sufferings, the travail of his soul, and the children of his love. It is theirs, for it is his. It is theirs, for they and he are one; they in him, and he in them. It is theirs, for his glory is their glory; his interests are their interests; and his heirship is their heirship. It is theirs, for *as* the Father loveth the Son, *so* the Son loveth them who are his; and as the Father hath delivered all things unto the Son for his control and gift, so the Son hath given all things unto them for their present and endless reward.

Let me state this whole matter in a more concise form.

All things are *devoted* to those who are *devoted* to the Lord Jesus Christ. If we are *his* servants, then every object and event is made *our* servant. If we seek to be productive of his highest *glory*, then he seeks to *make* every thing productive of our highest *enjoyment;* and every thing is so, in very deed; every thing without exception; every thing great and small, good and evil, past, present, and to come, spiritual and temporal, here and there and everywhere. In what other sense *all* things can be said to belong to those who belong to Christ, — in what other sense all things can be *theirs*, — it is difficult to conceive. If we are indeed Christ's in the best sense, if we were to become his as purely and as steadily as the angels in heaven, — would all things become ours in the way of *possession;* or rather, of *control?* How was it with the Corinthian church? They had no control of the wealth of the world, nor of the men of the world, nor of the gifts of the ministry of the Gospel, nor of their own life or death, nor of things present, nor of things to come. Yet *all* things were *theirs.* In what sense? Evidently in the only remaining sense, — devoted to them; their servants; controlled *for* them; overruled each, and all, and evermore, for their best and enduring happiness; overruled *so that,* out of every object and every event, *something* should be educed tributary, not only to their spiritual *perfection,* but to their *enjoyment.* From every mystery of Divine government, as from a deep sea, should come up for them some beauteous pearl; from every lurking-place of sin, as from the bowels of a mine, some precious stone; and from behind every cloud of judgment and retribution, even, some enrapturing form of wondrous glory.

But to avoid misapprehension of this truth let us look at it a little more closely.

Jesus Christ as God *manifest;* as the only communication or display of the Divine Being; aside from whom the Divine Excellence is "unapproachable," and unperceivable, and mantled with "clouds and darkness"; — I say, Jesus Christ, as the *manifestation* of God, is the "bread of Life." He is the aliment of the soul. In other words, the *affectionate perception* of the excellence of the Godhead shining *in him* is the only method of happiness for any created soul. To behold clearly and with *perfect* love, the fulness of God in the Son — is heaven. Every fresh display of this Divine fulness is an increase of heavenly enjoyment. Every thing which is *a means* of this display, is a means of new enjoyment to the soul who is beholding that fulness with *affection.* Now every thing *shall be* a means of unfolding "the glory of God, as it shines in the face of Jesus Christ." In some way, *every thing* shall illustrate the excellence of God; *every thing* shall furnish proof of the goodness of Him who orders and overrules every thing. Every thing *does* so; so far as it is understood by the creature. Every thing, therefore, being an interpreter of God's goodness, is a ministering servant to him who *loves* that goodness; and must be; and shall be; and shall ever be. And he who is "Christ's," who is devoted to him, *does* love that boundless goodness shining out in him; loves it more than all things else. It is his bread. It is his soul's aliment. It is his heaven. Every thing shall interpret to *him* that goodness. Every thing shall whisper to *him* some moving proof of Christ's glory. Every thing shall be as a cloud to distil upon *his* table the manna and the dew of spiritual Life, to impart to *his* soul thrift, and vigor, and enjoyment.

But — shall he feed and thrive upon the story of men's *woes* from generation to generation! Shall he *delight* in the abomination of his own and of others' sins! Shall the groans and the curses of hell be his gladness! Shall he revel in the smoke of others' torment! If so, where would be his delight in that God who hateth sin, and hath *no* pleasure in the death of the sinner? If so, — while God is what he is, — where would be his heaven? No. No. Impossible. Absurd.

Yet every thing is a ministering servant to those who are Christ's. In what way, then? In *this* way. The *terrific* things which you find in the history of the world, which you will find in the woes of hereafter, — without bating one jot of their terrors, without waking one pulsation of pride or exultation or brutal passion, — will so interpret *God*, will so unfold *his holiness*, will so lay open the unfathomed depths of his glory, that they who are Christ's shall be taught the more fully of the glories of their Redeemer by every tale of terror, by every bellowing wave of retribution, by every ebb and flow of depravity. There is no delight for them in others' guilt or woe. All their delight, and all their heaven, is — *God shining forth in Christ;* God *interpreted* by every terror as truly and as clearly as by every blessing. *Thus* it is that, to Christ's people, all things yield enjoyment; not as beauteous or delightful in *themselves* always, but *as interpreters of God;* as giving explanation or illustration, in some way, of that *most* wondrous Divine glory, — the work of Redemption by the Son.

In this wealth of the believer, what Grace! Here is the Grace of God going out in one ceaseless flow; expanding into one vast and beautiful ocean without a shore. O, it is all grace! it is *all* grace! Look at it; look at it, Christian believer; look at it and adore. If you are Christ's, — and, if a believer in him, you are, — if you have in sincerity brought yourself to his baptism; if you are trying to use your time and your privileges and your talents in his service, — then "all things are *yours*"; pledged to you; given to you; made and shaped and overruled to be tributaries to your purest and endless enjoyment. Every thing is to become a hewn stone in the fabric of your heavenly mansion; or a polished jewel in your crown of glory; or a savory viand in your banquet-house of Love.

How is it to-day? When you look upon the verdure of the fields; when you walk abroad under the bright and gladdening light of the sun; when you are compassed about by the heavenly stillness and the choice comforts of successive Sabbaths; when you see your children, as olive-plants, about your table, clad, and fed, and cared for, and bright with health, and hope, and promise; when you slake your thirst and refresh your spirit at earthly fountains opening and streaming all around you; and when you pluck the rich lusters of your common bounties, is there not in each, for *you*, some foretaste of heaven? Has not each, for *you*, a relish unknown to those who know not Christ? When you think of Him who is the Giver; when you look upon them as borne to you by *his* hand, as ministered to you by *his* love, is it not with subduing and blissful emotions? There — there — you recognize in every beauty and bounty of Nature, in the sacred rest of every Sabbath, in every precious tie of kindred, in short, in *every* good thing, something *more* than its own blessing, and its own loveliness There, in each, you behold mirrored, and mapped out, before you the loving-kindness of God. They stir up your heart to gladness, not because of their own richness only, but because in each you have a smile from heaven, — a token of remembrance, — a word of fellowship. They gladden you because they are good; but they gladden you *more* because they teach you, and prove to you, the goodness *of God.* Each new blessing, and each new day of blessings, gives you a new and deeper and clearer insight into his excellence.

So with the dark and gloomy things of life. When you think of His overruling power, you can hear, and you do hear, for your peace and comfort, a voice in every tempest, you see a handwriting upon every cloud, — "It is I, — it is I, — be not afraid." And when the wind has passed and the cloud overblown, you have found some spot upon your surrounding landscape, or upon your wayward heart, which has drunk a blessing; some spot whose brightness and newness of life have betokened the goodness of your God.

And how will it be with you hereafter? Why! if Paul's words are true, — just so then. No, — not *just* so then. Now — all things show you God so far as you study them and understand them. Then — all things *shall* show you God in the face of Jesus Christ *without fail;* for look at all, and understand all, you *will.* Then — *all* things shall unfold to you your God and your Saviour, just as *some* things, in your most precious and heavenly hours, do now. The same work which is wrought in you when the good things of providence, of the Gospel, and of the cross reveal to you anew the beauties of Christ, and knit your heart to him anew, — the same gladness, the same near access to the mercy-seat, the same dearness of communion, — shall *hereafter* be wrought in you by *all* things. Yes, — by all that have been, or are, or are to be. Now — you taste the cup; then — you shall drink at the fountain. Now — you hear sometimes a solitary note of melody sounding your Redeemer's goodness; but then — all things shall blend together in one ceaseless, rapturous chorus to make known his glory.

Who *are* ye, — to whom all things shall minister? Who *are* ye, — to whom all things shall interpret the glory of your best beloved? for whose service and bliss all things are enrolled and enlisted and pledged? Has never an impure breath ruffled the surface of your spirits? Have they always imaged the likeness of your God? Has never a thought, a wish, a passion, throbbed there, but with the sanction of the Law? Has never an affection moved with undue, unbalanced, forbidden strength? Has your best love *always* been for heaven? for God? Have your lives always been devoted to him? your bodies? your souls? Are you *deserving* of good at his hands, that he has made over to you this store of wealth, — *all* things? Deserving! of good! What say your consciences? What said the law when it served as your schoolmaster? when it taught you its lessons, and gave you experience of its scourgings? What say you, as you call to remembrance the wormwood and the gall? *What* say you, as you look now upon your hearts? Deserving — of good — at the hands of the *Lord!* Deserving — of all this! Why! brethren beloved, if you and I *are* Christ's, we were not *always* his. No, — O, no! We *have* thought, and spoken, and felt, and loved, not with deference to the law and the will of God, — but as we have pleased We let the law go. And we let God go. We loved pleasures and our fellow-creatures rather than God. And thus we sold ourselves to sin; broke the *whole* law; became corrupted through and through; stamped, dyed, leavened with sin; the very opposite of God. And we went on so; and we went on; and we *would go on;* against all the warnings of heaven; against all the arguments, and appeals, and provisions of Redeeming Love; against ten thousand admonitions and remonstrances of conscience; against the repeated rebukes and strivings of the Holy Spirit. We were "desperately wicked." Are WE deserving of good at the hand of the Lord? Are we deserving of "all things" as our inheritance? We are *deserving* enough; but it is of wrath, not of kindness; of everlasting beggary, not of riches; of hell, not of heaven. And we have felt this: in our very souls we have been *taught* it. We are not deserving of good; not of the least good; not of a moment of quietude; not of a crumb from the table of providence; not of a drop of refreshing mercy; not of a ray of hope.

Yet "all things" are ours. How? By what means? By what tenure? It is of God. It is of *grace.* It is by the *grace of God.* It is *all* of the grace of God. Witness the sins of our lives, — back — back — to childhood. Witness the domineering, lawless corruptions of our hearts. This wealth given to us is of grace in every part and portion, and in every moment of its duration. The vast fabric of our inheritance is written all over, from corner-stone to key-stone, with — "Grace — grace — unto it." And *such* grace! It is amazing! It is measureless! It *is* — matchless!

But this is not a dumb doctrine. It speaks. It speaks as with a thousand tongues. It speaks with all the eloquence and emphasis of heaven. It speaks; and its words are echoed from world to world, from congregation to congregation, by every thing that hath life, or form, or name, where the Spirit of God has brooded, or the purpose of God has been known. It calls aloud for our *tribute.* It calls upon those who are Christ's to make some return to him who has covenanted with them and for them. It is, as it were, the finger of

God pointing to the signet-mark upon the charter of Redemption, and to all things that are, and that are to be; to the magnificence of Divine bounty, to every fluttering hope, and every gushing enjoyment of the Christian's experience, appealing by all and in the name of all to the heir of these riches, and urging him to proper acknowledgments of his infinite obligations.

The wealth bestowed so richly, so freely, upon Christ's people, is reason for their rejoicing. Here indeed is cause for gladness. Here are "durable riches." And here, in this very bestowment, is distinct and surpassing proof of what God is. Here, in this very fact, is a fresh interpreter of God; gathering the *separate* testimony of all things into *one;* into one focal point of burning and overpowering glory.

But the doctrine of this rich inheritance argues for something *more* than joy. It argues for the tribute unto God of a lowly mind. Should we be puffed up as we look at the largeness and richness of his bounty to usward? Should we be puffed up because he has pledged to us all things? He has not done it because we are good. He has not done it because we are the least among sinners. In this bounty there is no proof, no intimation of good desert in us. No. Here is grace. Its *glory* is — its *grace.* Here, then in this bestowment of all things is something which points us, not only to the fulness and glory of God, but to the pollution in which he found us; to the hole of the pit whence he digged us; to our low estate and misery, when "by adoption" he made us heirs. "Where is boasting then? It is excluded"; excluded by that which is the very glory of our inheritance, — its *grace.* Thus, while we look at its splendor, while we are lost in surveying its wonders, we are forbidden *by it* to glory save in the Lord. We are commanded and compelled *by it* to bow with self-abasement, while we rejoice in the riches of grace. If these riches are ours, and if they are of grace, then our proper place is in the dust; our proper spirit is that of deep and eternal humility. The moment we look upon this inheritance with an emotion of self-glorying; the moment we make it an occasion of high looks or haughty thoughts, — we *pervert* it. It was given indeed for our *enjoyment.* But it was also given to make known and magnify, perpetually, the riches of God's grace. And while we look at this gift of "all things," if we *do* forget the guilt and the beggary in which he found us, we honor neither the gift nor the Giver. And is *this* a right return when the gift is *all* grace? Is *this* right, when its grace is its very peculiar glory? Why! its purpose, and argument, and very meaning, are all set aside except we see and own our vileness. Shall *we* do this? *We* who have come (we hope) to such an heirship! *We* whom God (we hope) has brought thither! Shall we? Can we? No. We must have our eyes and hearts open always, not only to the splendor and fulness of our inheritance, but to the wonder and glory of its grace; to the deeds and ill-desert of our fearful and desperate depravity *upon which* that grace is *based* and *upreared.*

But we owe to God another duty in return, — *service.* We always should have owed him this, had he never pitied, had he never redeemed, had he never sought us. Had he never shed upon us the blessings of his forbearance, of his tender providence, of his restraining grace; had he never given us *one* token of loving-kindness; we should have owed him entire and eternal service. How much more do we owe it now! How much more, — when he *has* pitied, and redeemed, and found, and blessed! O, *how* much more when he has bound us to Christ by renewing grace! *How* much more when he has bound *all* things in our service! when he has bidden *all* things to be our ministers! when he has opened for us fountains of living waters everywhere!

O my brother in Christ,—look! The argument of this bounty, the pealing argument of all this grace, is for *service.* Every thing is given to you! Yes,—and *every* thing adjures you to be *wholly* the Lord's. Shall such bounty, shall such grace, be powerless? You are beholden for steadfast, untiring, and unreserved service; not for a fitful, sluggish, wavering effort in the service of Christ. You are beholden for your time, for the vigor of your body, for the vigor of your mind, for the fervent love and obedience of your soul. You are told so by the precious truth before us. You are told so by every enjoyment of God which Nature, and Providence, and the Bible, and the Holy Spirit, and your closet, give you. You are told so in the name of every thing which can and shall display God's goodness; in the name of every thing which is to meet you in heaven as an interpreter of his glory. And will *you* waver in your love and devotedness to Christ! Will *you* divide your service between him and the world! Will *you* allow the dross, and the trash, and the lying vanities of life, to make you forget *his* loveliness and loving-kindness and grace! Will *you* be a stupid, slumbering, dronish disciple! *You!* before whom Christ has placed the sacred pledges of his redeeming, his covenanting, his unchanging love! written upon every thing that is, or has been, or shall be! *You!* an heir of God! a "joint heir with Christ"! an heir of "all things"! *You!* only yesterday a beggar, — a sinner, — an heir of death, — a "child of wrath"! to-day, with the priceless legacy of Almighty Grace in your hand! "Is this the kind return, are *these* the thanks, you owe?" Back, — back, — again I say, — look back to your nakedness and to your filthy state before your adoption. Compare what you were, with what you are; your hope of to-day, with your desert of damnation yesterday; the curse of your spiritual death, with the blessing of your spiritual resurrection; the midnight of your condemnation, with your present morning of unclouded grace! Does all this argue for a partial or a feeble service of your Redeemer? Is all this a plea or an apology for worldly-mindedness?

No. No. In the name of *grace,* — in the

name of that grace which is busy for you everywhere and for ever, which is culturing and culling enjoyments for you upon every spot where God reigneth, — in the name of your hope and your inheritance, — I adjure you be the Lord's *wholly*, *steadily*, cheerfully, for ever. *This* is your duty. *This* is the argument of the precious truth before you.

But give him *more*. *Praise* him. *Speak* of his wondrous grace. *Sing* of his boundless gifts. Be joyful in God, all ye his people; and let your joy break forth into songs. Let the harp be struck *to-day;* for the dayspring of your salvation has already come. Let his name be magnified and his grace be proclaimed by all who are the Lord's. Let it be done openly, loudly, always. O, give him this! Surely such grace has claim to such return. Surely goodness and bounty which go out without limit and without end should be sung on earth as well as in heaven. Praise the Lord, then, before all people. Let all men know that you adore him. Never let a blush be found upon *your* cheek; never let a denial come up to pollute *your* lips; when you are charged with belonging to Jesus of Nazareth. But commend him, praise him, for his grace, for his bounty, for his gifts to *you*, — a sinner.

It is *the least* you can do, to praise him with your lips, to praise him by the integrity and holiness of your life. And you are *told* to do it; told to, by the broad and sacred and solemn pledges of his outbursting love; told to, in the very words, "*All things are yours.*"

O, look, brother! The fulness of his grace is mirrored to you everywhere! The tokens of his love are sparkling in every fountain of your earthly relations. They are warming you and gladdening you in every sunbeam. They are smiling to you in every beauty of nature. They are beckoning to you mutely, but eloquently, in every twinkling star above you. Perhaps you do not hear and see to-day, but you will hereafter. *Then* these things, and other things, and "all things," will come up before you in memory or by revelation; and they will make heavenly music, each and all, in proof and praise of your Redeemer's kindness. Out of every event shall come something to make *him* manifest, and to make *you* full of heavenly rapture.

Now, then, with riches pledged to you in "all things," — with all the treasures of your beloved before you as the dowry of your espousals, — give him what you can and ought. Give him the beautiful offering of a humble spirit. Give him *constancy* in love and servic Give him *open praise.*

"Praise God, from whom all blessings flow;
Praise him, all creatures here below;
Praise him above, ye heavenly host,—
Praise Father, Son, and Holy Ghost."

X.

THE RECOGNITION OF CHRIST'S GRACE, — A DUTY.

Every thing which contributes to our comfort, whether an intrinsic good, or merely a preventive of evil, is of grace. Are we "born of God"? Are we enjoying the various privileges of adoption? Do our worldly interests, the institutions of the Gospel, or more direct Divine influences, suppress the fearful tendencies of our unrenewed hearts? Are we cheered by our domestic relations? Are we fed, and clothed, and sheltered? Do we enjoy health, and light, and air, and ten thousand objects of sense? Is there any thing — however minute — which exempts us from perfect misery? In each and all these things we receive "the manifold grace of God." To draw a single breath without pain, to experience the meanest sensation of fleshly delight, is as truly a matter of Divine grace, as to be "renewed in the spirit of our minds."

Having sinned, we deserve no blessing. Every blessing which we do receive is — grace.

Whether it be spiritual or temporal; whether special or common; whether great or trivial; it is unmerited, — it is forfeited, — it is of grace. Yet it is commonly understood that grace is concerned only in such blessings as regeneration, sanctification, salvation, and their several accompaniments. Men who talk loud and fervently of grace in *these* things, are often blind and dumb and dead to it as displayed in the little mercies of every day. They can see its glory in the cross, but do not detect it in the flower, in the dew, in the hour of peaceful repose or social fellowship. To some it would seem frivolous, if not profane, to apply so high an attribute of God to the painting of a flower, to the music of a bird, or to the texture of a garment. Yet it is wrong to *confine* our idea of God's grace to blessings pertaining to the soul. It is wrong; for, if it was grace which shone on the cross, if it is grace which is displayed in salvation, then it is grace which shines and speaks, and calls for praise in *all* the mercies of *all* the world.

Men readily acknowledge the more conspicuous truths of the Bible as articles of credence. They recognize, speculatively at least, the holiness and supremacy of God. The believer in Christ apprehends the severity and justice of the Law, and the fulness of the Redeemer, and the grace and glory and value of Redemption, — so far, at least, as the great sacrifice of atonement is concerned; and he anticipates with cheering hope the heavenly income of that Redemption. But where do you find a man, even among the most devout, who has uncovered, and studied, and revelled in, this truth, that "of the fulness of Jesus Christ have *all* we received, and grace for grace," i. e. grace upon grace? How many disciples of Jesus are there who think and *feel* that they are recipients of "his fulness" in any other way than as joint proprietors of atoning blood, and heirs apparent of a felicitous inheritance? How many who remember and *feel* that they receive "of the fulness" of their Redeemer, that they pluck and eat the fruits of *his* sufferings, that they are gladdened and refreshed by the ministrations of *his* hands, every day and hour and moment? How many, think you, are there in this wide world, — in this ransomed world, — who see the footprints of Jesus in their pathway? who catch the voice of his benediction in the events of their histories? who discern the impress of his hand, and the badges of his love, and the memorials of his baptism, in *all* things?

Countless, ceaseless, are the gifts of his grace to *all* the tenants of this world of hope. And countless are the gifts of his grace which are taken, and enjoyed, and eagerly consumed, without a thought of their sacredness, or an acknowledgment of their source. They are rich. They are profuse. They are omnipresent. They are, as it were, an innumerable company of angels, declaring his goodness, unfolding his love, and chanting his praises, to whose voices scarcely an ear is turned or a tongue responds.

Is this right? Do we quit ourselves of duty when we overlook and slight an evidence, a fruit, or a memorial of Redeeming Love? Is it right to slight the testimony of Jesus in the Bible? Is it right to disregard the fountain of Redeeming blood? Is it right to turn our backs upon the sacramental board? Where, and what, is the gift of Christ, — where, and what, is that one thing, great or small, which comes to us in *his* name and from *his* hand, yet deserves no recognition as a token of his Love?

Grace through Christ is our choicest treasure. It is a sacred treasure. It is as sacred in the eye of God as his own name, and honor, and integrity. And while he watches with jealousy its reception by us, can we meet it and take it and use it unmindful of its value and its origin, yet do no wrong? We have no more right to draw a veil over God's most glorious attribute when displayed in that which is least, than when displayed in that which is greatest. We have no more right to spurn it in a petty providence, than in the matchless deed of Redemption. No! whatever form that grace may assume, we are bound to recognize it; to recognize it *as* the grace of Christ. Whether it be reflected to us from Sinai, or from Calvary, or from a thousand inferior things, matters nothing. In any kindness which God shows us, we ought to detect his agency. We should receive such a blessing, — no matter what it is, — feeling that it is *his* gift; feeling that it is undeserved, that, being undeserved, it is a gift of his grace. Not only should we know and remember that it is from his hand, but we should do so with emotion. It should be received devoutly. While we detect his superscription upon it, we should do so with filial hearts. We should delight in it, not so much for the gift's sake as for the Giver's; not so much in the blessing as in the grace of the blessing. Let us enjoy it. Let us be ravished with it, if we will. But *through* the blessing let us discern *the grace* — humbly, heartily, affectionately, — and *in* the grace behold the image of the Giver, and trace his precious care and love. "It is a gift, — a gift from heaven, — a gift of grace," — should be the tribute of our lips, the fervent acknowledgment of our hearts. *Thus* should we receive the gift; *thus* recognize the grace.

But as such gifts are repeated, our recognition of grace should be repeated. We should render this tribute *habitually;* for the blessings of to-day, — for the blessings of to-morrow, — for the blessings of yesterday. If grace assume a thousand forms, and write its name upon ten thousand objects, — then a thousand and ten thousand times should we perform this duty. Let not one blessing slip by without welcoming it in the name, and as the grace, of heaven. Taste not a cup of mercy, — nay, not a drop thereof, — without relishing the love and the grace which commingle in it. And when the cup is drained, when the gush of enjoyment is over, let the grateful memory of it be cherished. If we would fully recognize the grace which blesses us, we must treasure up the past; we must keep a catalogue of our mercies; we must hallow that catalogue in our hearts.

It is neither fit to overlook grace as it passes before us, nor to forget it when it is past.

I have said that we receive grace to an extent coequal with our blessings. What, then, are our blessings? and are they all of grace?

There are blessings peculiar to the believer. Christian brother, — you love God. Yes, though that love be faint and flickering, yet — if your name be not a false one — you love God. But have you always loved him? No. But a little while ago you shut your heart against him. You cringed and bowed at the altar of some earthly idol. You "worshipped and served the creature more than the Creator." But a little while ago, and you was a doubter of God. You did not and would not confide in his Word, or his Sovereignty, or his dealings. Your feet were upon his statute-book. Your heart was full of evil. You nursed your corruptions; and they grew. You so tutored your depravity that you could quench the Holy Spirit, and withstand Redeeming Love. But the veil is removed from your heart. You have felt the infusion of a new principle. This hatred of a holy God has passed away. Your lips have sung praises, and your heart has melted beneath the cross of Christ. Have you forgotten the love of your espousals? Have you forgotten the wormwood and the gall? Have you forgotten your deliverance?

And are *you* pardoned? Are *you* a new creature? Do *you* bear the image of God? Is the seal of Redemption upon *your* soul? upon yours, where but yesterday was the peculiar sin of despising and rejecting Christ? Yesterday greedy for husks, and chaff, and vanity, — now with a "hope full of immortality"! Yesterday gazing, with idolatrous delight, upon the sparkling frailties which will be burned up to-morrow, — now with your eye upon a crown of life! Yesterday a "child of perdition," — to-day a child of God! Yesterday a slave of sin, — now an heir of glory!

And to what privileges are you admitted? To the privilege of endearing fellowship with Christ; of communing with him as friend communeth with friend; of *feeling* the presence and sympathy and consolations of your best beloved; of thus having on earth a foretaste of heaven. To the privilege of that "hope which is as an anchor to the soul." To the privilege of that faith which is Life eternal. To the privilege of "the peace of God which passeth all understanding." To the privilege of sanctified afflictions. All these are yours, in proportion to your fidelity, and your intimacy with Christ.

Precious, precious blessings! fitted to the soul! to its helplessness,—its pollution,—its wretchedness,—its immortality!

How came they yours? Did you earn them? Did you sow their seed? Did *you* break up the soil on which they have grown? Did *you* conquer the thorns and briers which grew in riot there before? No. *Your* seed was the teeth of dragons; and the harvest would have been after its kind. Well; how came you to be a new creature? How came such a one as you were to love God? to sit at the foot of the cross? to taste Redeeming love? to enjoy the privileges consequent upon spiritual adoption? Was the work yours? No,—no. Christ wrought it; not you. "You love him because he *first* loved you." "You did not choose him, but he chose you."

Then these spiritual blessings are *gifts*. But were they merited? Yes;—if sin merits blessings; if pollution merits the fellowship and embrace of purity; if rebellion merits pardon; if depravity merits heaven; then you have merited the privileges and heirship of your adoption.

O, look at the comforts of a believer in Christ! See them in all their forms of beauty. Behold their subduing, heavenly influences. Witness their effects through the vicissitudes of life; through the conflict — that victorious conflict — with death. Look at that spiritual change of his, by which he is introduced to these blessings. Look at what he *was*, — at what he *is*. Surely they are not deserved. Surely they are not earned. Every one of them is of grace. In germ, in bud, in blossom, in ripeness, in bestowment, in enjoyment, — they are each and all and altogether — grace.

There are blessings which believers and unbelievers receive in common.

Suppose, now, there were no verdant fields throughout the world; and no flowers; and no breath of wind to waft their fragrance; and no pleasant sounds to greet our ears. Suppose the sun were blotted out; and the moon; and the stars. Suppose there were no form of beauty, and no source of bodily delight around us. Suppose all the *superfluities* of external nature were swept away, and nothing left to us but the mere essentials of animal existence. Are we aware how much enjoyment we receive from the myriads of objects which address our senses? Are we aware how a thousand neglected beauties, and ten thousand unnoticed springs of comfort, are silently dropping their contributions of kindness upon our hearts? Rain, and sunshine, and pure air, and the singing of birds, and the beauty of flowers, and the mute splendor of the stars, are little thought of. But men who have been bereft of them — and such men there have been — have thought much of them; and have pined, and groaned, and cursed, and died, in misery for the want of them.

But this is only one department of our temporal blessings. There is our table, spread to nourish us. There is our raiment, to protect us. There are our dwellings, to shelter us. There are our fields and our flocks and our herds, our silver and our gold, our beds, our friends, our nights of rest, our mornings of vigor and health. There are our family enjoyments; parental, filial, fraternal, conjugal affection and sympathy and communion, — with their unnumbered seasons of refreshing. There are our providential bounties, of endless variety and of hourly recurrence. Are all these things trivial? Are they unworthy to be mentioned? Let them depart, — and there would come upon you a night of desolation whose darkness would be terrific. A blight would come over you whose influence defies conception.

Here, then, is this bounteous furniture of nature, — here are these countless ministrations of providence, — showering their precious blessings upon us with the revolution of every year and of every moment. However we may have labored to secure them, yet we know that we have not *earned* them. A wind, a breath, the slightest accident, might defeat the toil and labor and calculation of years. We cannot guaranty to ourselves the slightest blessing. We cannot put our finger on a single bounty and say, — "*It is ours.*" No; they are *gifts.* From some source or other, — they are gifts.

Are they by right, or — by bounty? Are they by right, or — by grace? Why! if we have an angel's purity; if we are unsullied by a single breath of sin; if not a thought contrary to the law has crept over our hearts; — then they are by *right.* But if *one* transgression be written against us, then they are of *grace.* If one impure wish has left its traces upon our souls, — it was the forfeiture of *all* blessing.

Need I tell or prove our demerit? It is written on our consciences. We know it. We feel it. Then I need not argue out *the grace* which signalizes our blessings. I need only say, that by *every* sin, and by *every* pollution within us, the grace which surrounds us, which sanctifies the various good things of life, is enhanced. And if the grace be increased as demerit is increased, how great, how wondrous, how magnificent, the grace which creates and gives all this congregation of mercies!

But there are also blessings peculiar to unbelievers.

They are beset with influences whose direct design and tendency is to turn them from the misery and emptiness of a worldly mind, to the peace and satisfaction of a spiritual mind; from feverish, discontented unbelief, to healthful, happy faith. Such are their Bibles, — their Sabbaths, — their sanctuary privileges, — the strivings of the Spirit with their hearts. These are the only stars of hope which glimmer upon their future prospects. If these prevail not over unbelief, the sinner is beyond help.

But more; that unbelief is the comprehen

sive element of utter woe. Joined with it, — combined with it, — there are attributes of character and faculties of soul whose full development is perfect ruin. Look at unbelief, — that spirit of distrust toward God, that disagreement with God's will, that chafing dislike of his government. It has a demoniac power. It has power to scathe the soul with unutterable torments. To-day, — it only murmurs against God. It is only a little restive when the Law rebukes it. It is only a little fretful when it feels God's sovereignty. It is only slightly moved when the providence of God thwarts its plans and cuts off its worldly hopes. But these light ripplings of unbelief mar the sinner's peace. And if *these* mar his peace, what, — *what*, I ask, would be the spiritual havoc of that same unbelief, should it reign in all its despotic might and fury? Let it come in contact with the will of God at every point; let it feel the supremacy and power of God at every turn; let it cross the purposes of God at every moment; let it contend against the plans and deeds of God perpetually and with all its might; and the unbeliever's whole experience would be frenzy, madness, despair. This is not supposition only. Unbelief — like every other habit of the soul, whether good or bad — is capable of indefinite progression and indefinite power.

Add to this development of unbelief, the power of a guilty conscience. In all his impotent conflicts with God's will and might, let the unbeliever see God's holiness; let him feel that God is right and he is wrong; let him feel that all his history has been black with guilt from the first pulsation of his unbelief onward, — and here are a thousand stings darting their venom upon his soul perpetually, and without an antidote.

O, there are fire and fuel in the unbeliever's heart which only a breath would fan into a devouring flame; which need the influence of only a breath to consume every semblance of enjoyment, to silence every profession of peace, to lick up every vestige of pride, — for ever!

Such are the unbeliever's inbred curses; the elements of death which are in ambush in his heart. But what are his blessings? His blessings! The *checks which restrain* these curses. *Why* does unbelief now work so slightly? *Why* does conscience now whisper so gently? They are held back. For *mercy's* sake, their power is fettered. They struggle against God, they war against the sinner's peace, as much as they can. They urge him as near to *perfect* depravity and to *perfect* misery as they can. But there are barriers around them which they cannot overleap. These barriers alone interpose between the unbeliever and despair.

Who has raised them up? The sinner? No. They are blessings. They are *gifts*, — put there by some one who knows his depravity, and desires his good, and dreads his misery, more than the unbeliever does.

O, *what* grace is restraining grace! The only separation-wall between unbelief and hell! All the influences at work for his conversion, and all the checks upon his depravity, come within the proper catalogue of the sinner's peculiar blessings. And they are each and all of grace. The very stigma of his unbelief *proves* them all of grace.

To what extent, then, is grace dispensed to us in our present state? To every possible extent. It stretches its span, and diffuses its gifts, over the whole field of our existence. Grace! it beams in every blessing. It sparkles in every cup of delight. It sits at every table. It smiles in every family of love. It is found in every spiritual enjoyment. It adorns every beauty of nature, and every bounty of providence. Its signet-mark is on the Sabbath, and on every Gospel privilege. And its strong seal is upon every impediment of unbelief. It is everywhere, where there is a comfort for the human heart, or an abatement of human sorrow.

Then it should be *recognized* — everywhere. We should see it, and praise it, and enjoy it, in all our mercies; on every hand; at every step; in every hour.

But why should we recognize this grace as *Christ's?*

Because it *is* his. Because the savor of *his* Love, and the print of his finger, are upon every blessing.

Who is their source? Whose hand arched the heavens, and lit their lamps, and made and clothed the world? Who filled the mines of Nature with their exhaustless stores? Do you not know — who? He who "was in the beginning with God. All things were made by *him;* and without him was not any thing made that was made." He who "was made flesh and dwelt among us *full of grace* and truth."

I ask again, Who is Head over all things? Christ "is the head of all principality and power." He "is gone into heaven, and is on the right hand of God; angels and authorities and powers being made subject unto him." "All things are under his feet." "All things are delivered unto him of the Father." It is Jesus Christ, then, who controls the wheels of Nature. It is Jesus Christ who arranges all our circumstances in life; who allots to us providences, spiritual restraints, spiritual comforts.

But let it never, never, be forgotten, — we are sinners. It is our sin which *makes* our blessings — grace. From our first sin we were obnoxious to punishment; we were *deserving* of nothing else. Justice demanded — righteously demanded — curses upon our heads. But — we have been reprieved from punishment. Nay, — reprieve is not all. Reprieve has been one ceaseless, bounteous harvest-season of precious mercies. The tenderness of Christ has not had reference merely to our exposure to retribution. He has grasped at blessings, too; not merely at a blessing here and another there, but at blessings for us *all along;* at *profusion* of gifts; at the *best* of gifts. Is here no wrong to Justice? Can the Law, and government, and righteousness of God be "magnified and made honorable," — can his character be without blemish, —

while such blessings are bestowed upon sinners?

Brother, — the answer is in the cross of Christ. On that cross was made a sacrifice for sin. But for that sacrifice, Justice *must* have been wronged; God's government *must* have been impeached; his character *must* have been marred; by any deed of kindness towards us. Consequently, — had it not been for Christ's death, the anguish of his soul, the bitterness of his cup; had it not been that he trod "the winepress of the wrath of God," that he was "wounded for our transgressions and bruised for our iniquities," — not a deed of mercy, not a moment's respite from wrath, not an hour of blessing, not a beam of hope, not a smile of enjoyment, could have been given us. Justice *must* have cut us off, not only from spiritual blessing, but from carnal; not only from fellowship with God hereafter, but here; not only from the brightness of heaven, but from all brightness, all cheerfulness, all sources of enjoyment, in *this* world.

Has Christ, then, made all things which are fitted to our enjoyment, and which we do enjoy from day to day? Has he the sovereign control of all things which are made? and of us? Has he the management of every wind, and the dispensation of every good? Does *he* give us life and breath and all things? *Does* he cheer the believer? *Does* he adorn the world around us? *Does* he give with his own hand every providential blessing? *Does* he restrain the depravity of unbelief? Yes.

But where gets he his warrant? Whence comes his right? He *bought* it. He bought it at the hand of Justice. He paid for it a price, — the highest price the universe could furnish. It was not silver. It was not gold. It was his own precious blood. It was "his *soul*, — an offering for sin."

Brother, — *the cross of Christ* is the source of our blessings. The cross of Christ — is the fountain-head of *all* grace. The anguish of its Sacrifice was the price of our gifts.

Well, then; the *impress* of that cross is upon every good thing. The gifts of Nature, of Providence, the Bible, the Sabbath, the Sanctuary, the privileges of adoption, the manifold checks upon depravity, all — all — are the purchases of Redemption. Not a comfort do you enjoy; not a moment do you consume; not a form of beauty do you behold; not a glow of health do you feel; you have not a night of rest, not a day of brightness, not a child, not a garment, not a dollar; but it is a memorial of Redeeming Love. The name of Christ, — the love of Christ, — the death of Christ, — are portrayed before you everywhere. The signet-mark of *Redemption* is on your tables, your cups, your furniture, your door-posts, your fireside, your harvests, your family fellowship.

We ought, also, to recognize *as Christ's* the grace displayed in all our mercies; because such recognition makes all things our servants.

It makes them peculiarly tributary to *our enjoyment.* It matters not how slender is your purse, how mean your table, or how humble your home. Look upon each as the gift of Christ; look upon each as better than you deserve; look upon each as procured for you by the high price of atonement; look upon each as a memorial of Redeeming Love; look upon each as a mercy for which praise and gratitude are due, and feel the gratitude and speak the praise; and every individual bounty will fill your heart with life. You will welcome home, and food, and income, not for their own sakes only, but because they bear the image and superscription of Divine affection, of Redeeming Grace.

Have you not something in your possession which is associated in your mind with the memory of an absent, or a departed friend? Something which a parent gave you? or a brother? or a sister? or a husband? or a wife? I ask not whether it be a fortune, or a trinket. It is a gift of affection. It is a memorial of one who is gone. Yes; and *because* it is a memorial, — *because* it reminds you of the kindness and the virtues of one whom you esteem and love, — *because* it revives that particular image in your mind, — it is a treasure. Be it a diamond, or be it a bawble, it is a treasure; it is a source of *enjoyment.*

Such are all the blessings of life — the greatest and the least alike — to him who, with an affectionate heart, recognizes them as the gifts of Christ. They *are* memorials of your Redeemer. They *are* tokens of his love. Look upon them as such, — welcome them, prize them, as such, — suffer them to remind you of his grace, of his unspeakable love, of his "suffering of death," — then they are doubly precious; precious for their own sakes, but above all precious for *his* sake. They cheer you as blessings; but, above all, as reviving in your heart the image of that boundless love and matchless glory which reside in the person of your Redeemer. You *cannot but* rejoice in the relish of every fruit, in the beauty of every flower, in the dispensation of every good, if you *truly* perceive therein the grace and love of Christ. In your home, in your table, in your civil institutions, in your garden, in your field, in earth and sky, in day and night, in the Sabbath, in the sanctuary, and in all the orderings of providence, you will have sources of enjoyment which the purblind worldling knows nothing of. All these things will bestir in your heart those fervent emotions whose very exercise is happiness, — whose *perfect* exercise is heaven. The very reverses and bereavements which affect you will be channels of enjoyment, for you will perceive how they are attempered by grace; you will feel that, with all their sharpness, they are gentler than you deserve, and are made so by Redeeming Love.

I envy not the man who eats up the blessings of life as an ox does the grass of the field; with no relish beyond that of their sweetness. I envy not the man who tastes nothing upon his table but food; who sees nothing in the stars but light, and nothing in the revolutions of providence but changes of good or ill. He has his enjoyments, to be sure; but they are low, and narrow, and evanescent. But enjoyments such as he gathers who humbly and affectionately detects the impress of a Saviour's grace, and hears the whisperings of a Saviour's love, in every passing providence and in every object of nature, I do covet. Such are the enjoyments of heaven where *all* things are relished only as interpreters of Christ; where every angel and every pavement is brilliant only because "the glory of God doth lighten them, and *the Lamb* is the light thereof." *Such* enjoyments may be coveted by an earthly pilgrim.

But again, this recognition of Christ's grace "makes all things our servants," because it makes all things *fortify us against temptation.* There is no object of sense which may not seduce us to sin. Yet the power resides not in the *object*, but in the *subject.* That blessings and beauties are means of transgression, is not because there is inherent evil in them, but because the heart which looks upon them is in an evil mood. Correct the heart, — hold *that* in a right attitude and frame, — and you dissipate the temptation.

It is not when you are filled with a devout perception of the glory of Christ, that you are excited by any external thing to murmuring, or envying, or anger, or fraud. It is not when your heart is throbbing in gratitude and amazement in view of Redeeming Love; it is not when you are studying and adoring the unsearchable riches of grace, — that you give place to error of heart or behavior. It is when you forget these things. Read them, then, upon all things; make all things mementos of Christ; hear their testimony of his love; detect their relation to his cross; do this habitually; make the Bible, and the sanctuary, and providence, and nature, and hardships, and comforts, things high and things low, conduct your thoughts and heart to Him who arranges them all; look upon all things, and all events, as parts of a great and beauteous temple which He has reared, and wherein He dwells "full of *grace* and truth"; and you may walk the world over in safety.

Can you revile him who reviles you, if then that very wrong reminds you of the grace of Him who "reviled not again"? Can you covet your neighbor's goods, and overreach him in trade, when you *feel* that *Christ* makes you to differ, and that *Christ* has given you already more of goods than you deserve? Can you rail at a wicked man if his wickedness wakes you to a grateful remembrance of

One who died alike for him and for you? Can you misuse your property, or grudge to use it for good, while you feel, thankfully and humbly, that you hold it by grace? and that it is a product of Christ's death? Can you murmur and repine, that you have *only* a cottage for shelter, and *only* a crust for food, while in these very things you recognize the grace of Christ?

To suppose that you can do these things, is absurdity. It is supposing the same breath to utter blessing and cursing. It is supposing the same feeling to be good and evil.

No, brother beloved, — so far as you devoutly recognize that grace which characterizes all the mercies of life, just so far you neutralize the power of temptation. And if you thus recognize it everywhere and always, you clear your path of snares; so far as it affects *you*, you purge *the whole world* of temptation.

But yet again; this recognition of Christ's grace "makes all things our servants," because it makes all things *tributary to our perfection.* The Gospel of the *cross* is "the power of God unto salvation." The "truth as it is in *Jesus*" is the grand, efficacious means by which sinners are converted and sanctified. And though the *preaching* of the Truth stands preëminent in the system of means, yet it is *only* preëminent. In whatsoever way the truth in Christ is shadowed forth, — whether in baptism, or the Lord's supper, or providence, — that way is adapted to fit men for heaven. And in whatever object or event we recognize that truth devoutly, in that we have an aid to sanctification. That object, and that event, promote our holiness.

Now, then, the hand of Christ is in every natural object, and in every occurrence of life. In each, the dying love of Christ is concerned. Each speaks, then, of the truth as it is in him. Each brings you some lesson interpretative of the cross. You behold the object, or the event, and *therein* you also behold the Truth. You behold it devoutly, teachably. It has made its impression upon you. But what impression? It has wakened you to holy affections. It has given impulse, strength, growth, to those affections. And in the same degree it has weakened the power of indwelling sin. In other words, — by recognizing the grace of Christ in things around you, you have made them vehicles of Gospel truth, and therefore tributary to your ultimate perfection.

But look at the mode of this operation.

You sit down at your table to refresh your body with the bounty of Providence. As you receive the gift, — as you consider the cheerfulness and comfort of those who share your board, — as you enjoy the pleasures of domestic fellowship, — you remember that these comforts are the gifts of Christ. You call to mind that He has created the world and given it its increase; that He, overruling every event of providence, has spread that table, and ordained that family circle. You call to mind the truth, that, had not He interfered in your behalf by sacrifice, by blood, that hour of blessing would never have been your allotment, that therefore it is of *grace* and the purchase of his Love. Your thoughts and your heart go up from the gifts to the Giver, — from the things purchased to the price, — from the fleshly blessings to the cross; and thus with a spirit of fervent Christian gratitude you eat your bread, and drink your cup, and enjoy your social board. You have met *Christ* there. And the blessings before you have not been refreshment for the body merely, but for the soul. Recognizing *the grace of Christ* there, your heart has been impelled to heavenly emotions. You have been quickened in Divine life. You have been made to advance toward the fulness of the stature of perfection in Christ.

Use any other blessing in the same way, and the same influence is experienced. Use all things in the same way, and all things become tributary to your spotless resemblance to God.

But we ought also to recognize *as Christ's* the grace displayed in all our mercies, because if we do not, we sin.

Whether God speak to us, as to his people of old, by an audible voice, or in the silent language of the written Word, if we do not hear and heed and revere the voice, we sin. Whether he display himself by the visible symbol of the Shekinah, or by the visible glory of the natural heavens, if we do not reverently recognize that memorial of God, we sin. The Law is — God's. The heavens are — God's. The world and the fulness thereof are — God's. They speak in His name. They declare His glory. "In Christ's stead," they call upon us to respond, joyously and reverently, to their declarations. If we shut the ear, and lock up the heart, and give back no response; if we overlook this testimony of Christ; we trifle with *his* messengers and lightly esteem his glory.

Were we to pass through a host of angels, every one of whom had some different thing to say about the power and wisdom and holiness of "God in Christ"; and should we simply scan their forms and graces and vestments, but give no heed to their words, — surely we should sin; we should despise the revelation of Divine glory. But what matters it whether we pass thus listless and careless through a throng of preaching angels, such as bow and praise in heaven, or through a throng of angels, such as preach to us in the Word, in Providence, in Nature? What matters it *how* Christ is preached? What matters it by whom? (Philipp. i. 18.) If we spurn the sermon, do we not spurn the testimony? And if we spurn the testimony of Jesus, do we not sin?

But we were speaking of the *grace* of Christ. Now if it be a sin to overlook a manifestation of his power, or his holiness, or his wisdom, or his justice, much more is it a sin to treat lightly a manifestation of his grace. Grace is his *highest* glory. Grace is his *most sacred* attribute. Grace is the attribute in which all his other attributes converge. And when we look sleepily upon any memorial of his *grace*, we contemn the *whole assemblage* of his glories. If, then, we overlook the grace of Christ as displayed in His common mercies, we do so at our peril; we incur a fearful guilt.

But more; if we overlook the grace of Christ as displayed in our mercies, "we sin" by putting the mercy in the place of the Giver. You sit down and enjoy food and raiment and home and wealth and friends. You walk abroad cheered by the light of the sun, refreshed by the air of heaven, delighted by the fruits and flowers of the garden, or by the sparkling glories of an evening sky. You enjoy these things, but do not enjoy the grace which they portray. You open your heart to them, but not to their Creator and gracious Giver. You delight in them, but not as the gifts and memorials of grace. Yes, — and thereby you have installed the creature in the sanctuary of your affections, and have shut out the Creator. You have burned your incense upon the altar of the world, and withholden it from the altar of the Lord. You have embraced and appropriated, enjoyed and consumed, the blessing; unmindful, neglectful, of the Giver. The outgoings of your heart have stopped at the very point whence they should have risen up to Christ. The blessing is substituted for the Benefactor; the creature, for its Maker; the world, for God. The token of grace is *converted* into an *idol.* The sanctuary of your heart — where Christ ought to be — is polluted and desecrated. He is rifled of his dues, by the godless, graceless welcome which you have lavished on his bounty.

But this is not all. If you overlook his grace in your mercies, *you pervert it.* Those mercies, as the fruits of his grace, have their specific errand and design over and above your sensual comfort. They are not ordained and dispensed for the flesh merely. They are designed and fitted to be clews to the grace which they embody. They are intended as so many mediums of intercourse between yourself and your Redeemer; as so many ladders by which you should climb, as it were, to heaven; as so many telescopes through which you should spy out the manifold glory of Christ. They come to preach to you the Gospel. They come to remind you of the cross. They come as pledges of Redeeming Love. They come as remembrancers of Him who loved you before the world was. They come so to quicken your heart to love and devotion, so to attune it to grateful praise, that it shall be fitted for the harmony of heaven. Overlook their *grace*, — pass them by, just as though they had nothing to say or to show of Christ, — meet them just as though they were *not* the fruits of a Redeemer's sufferings, — and what do you do? You use grace as a tool for sin. You do not pass its blessings by. You do not simply let alone its monumental mercies. You *pervert* them. You take that which was meant for your spiritual good, and *make* it an instrument of spiritual pollution. The vessels of the Lord's temple are profaned at the altar of idolatry.

Are you afraid to come to the sacramental table because, if you "eat and drink not discerning the Lord's body," i. e. not recognizing his grace in Redemption, "you eat and drink damnation to yourself"? Brother, if you discern not his redeeming grace in your *common blessings*, you eat and drink damnation (condemnation, judgment) to yourself. The beauties of the external world and the events of providence are as *truly* memorials of a *crucified* Redeemer, as the sacramental bread and wine. *These* are *special* memorials; *those* are *common. These* are *typical* of atonement itself; *those* are *products* of atonement. This is the only difference. All are designed as remembrances of the grace of Christ. To be blind to his grace in one thing is as verily a sin, as to be blind to it in any other thing.

Behold, then, the reasons for a grateful, humble, hearty recognition of the grace of Christ in the common things and common events of life.

Every blessing is his gift; for he made and distributes all.

Every blessing has been bought for you — at the cost of his crucifixion.

To be alive to their testimony will make them fountains of heaven-like enjoyment.

It will shield you against sin.

It will make every mercy of life tributary to your sanctification.

If you recognize *not* the grace of Christ in your blessings, you sin; you sin, by lightly esteeming that grace; you sin, by making the blessings of grace your gods; you sin, by wresting grace to your own destruction.

My dear brother, — you are not *a brute.* Brutish enjoyments are not enough for you. You want those which are fitted to your *soul.* You need all possible consolations in such a world as this. You have sins enough already, and need every possible safeguard against new sins. You have corruptions enough already, and need every possible help to sanctification. I beseech you, then, look not upon the world and the things of the world as a brute does. Reckon not the enjoyments which are spiritual by the scale of a brutish judgment. Weigh not the pollutions of your heart in the balances of the flesh. But — with all the energy and earnestness of an immortal spirit, roused to a sense of its perils and its wants — search out the fountains of spiritual blessing, and the preventives of spiritual evil, which everywhere abound.

"Of Christ's fulness have all we received, and grace upon grace." His grace is everywhere; in the Bible; in the Sabbath; in the sanctuary; in the sacraments; in prayer; in the events of your life; in all the monuments of his power and skill and goodness which are around you. Go to every one for instruction. Go to every one, hungering and thirsting for spiritual bread and for living water. Go and unlock every casket of Divine glory. Go and search out, and recognize, and adore, the matchless grace of your Redeemer, wherever it is displayed. Pass no mercy and no beauty by, as though it were dumb and barren. Every one has its testimony of Jesus. And if you will but open your eye and your heart to *all* the disclosures of his grace, you will find all the world a book of revelation. You will find all Nature and all Providence chanting one perpetual anthem to his praise. You will find the universe an orchestra where ten thousand thousand tongues are singing of the wonders of the cross, and of the riches of its grace.

And if you devoutly recognize their speech, if you give daily, hearty heed to their varied testimony, you will make the world your servant, — you will make temptation your captive, — you will make the "forlorn-hope" of Satan a ministering angel to your soul.

But if you slight the revelation of your Saviour's grace which is brought to you in your daily mercies, — if you walk through this vast storehouse of his memorial gifts, unmoved by their testimony, — you must meet hereafter a condemning witness in every individual blessing. And when those witnesses tell how they appealed to you in vain, — how they could never touch your heart by their display of grace, — then will the Judge say, with fearful emphasis, and with fearful justice, too, — "I have called, but you have refused. I have stretched out my hand, but you have not regarded. Therefore I laugh at your calamity; I mock when your fear cometh." And, in the light of such testimony, of all the universe who bear Christ's image, none will gainsay the sentence; but every lip will cry, and every heart will echo back, — "Amen and Amen!"

O, then recognize grace in all things! in every star, and flower, and sunbeam; in every portion of bread; in every cruse of water. And, O, recognize their grace as *Christ's!* as the product of his power; as the gift of his hand; as the pledge of his love; as the purchase of his sufferings. *Do* not walk blindfold through this living host of Christ's witnesses. *Do* not hurry through these omnipresent memorials of Redeeming Love, — these dear-bought, hard-earned, sacred memorials of Redeeming Love, — with your ear deaf to their testimony, and your heart senseless to their appeals; for, as the light of the sun in the firmament doth gild and beautify every object in Nature, so do the power and operation of Christ — the light, and love, and overflowing grace of his cross — beam from the most trivial events of our lives.

XI.

THE BELIEVER'S DEBT TO CHRIST.

I KNOW not where or when we can stop, in numbering the glories of our Redeemer. I know not where or when we can stop in surveying the riches of his grace. I know not where or when we can stop in counting the number of his tender mercies, or in measuring the depths of his Love. I know not where or when we could stop, were we simply to undertake to show what he has done for those whom he has chosen out of the world. We need the noonday revelations of hereafter; we need to stand, with quickened vision, before the very Throne; we need to behold, face to face, eye to eye, the glory of Him who sitteth thereon; we need to behold and understand the sinfulness of sin, the pureness, the kindness, and the curse of the Law; we need to learn the mixture of that "cup of the winepress of the wrath of God"; we need to read the histories of those who shall be saved;—before we can have surveyed *the outlines* of His grace toward them. We want Eternity to tell the story, to describe the grace, and to utter equal praise.

Yes, brethren in Christ Jesus,—ye who were sometime without Christ, "strangers from the covenants of promise, having no hope, without God, who were far off but now are made nigh by the blood of Christ,"—in counting and describing what he has done *for you*, you might go on, and go on, from point to point, from view to view, from wonder to wonder, from praise to praise, and your theme would never fail; its beauties, its glories, its wonders, would never—never—*never* fade.

Come, then, and let us look at our personal obligations to Christ. You are *in debt* to him. You are indebted to him for many, for peculiar, for precious blessings; indebted to him for *more* than they who have not obtained like precious faith with you; indebted to him for distinguishing and inestimable favors. We cannot weigh, and understand, their multitude or magnitude. But *do* let us *look; do* let us *meditate;* do let us *revolve* those favors; *do* let us stand under the light of his loving-kindnesses; till our sluggish hearts beat once more with the fervor of our first love, with the subdued emotions of the day of our espousals.

For what are you indebted to Christ? For

what are you indebted to him *as a believer?* How are you indebted to him more than they who believe not? Their obligations to him are beyond estimate; but yours are yet greater. Theirs are such, that every moment's refusal to praise and serve him is fearful sin; but yours are more and greater.

You are indebted to Christ for Redemption. "He is the Saviour of all men; *specially* of them that believe." His sacrifice was sufficient for all; and, in many precious ways, available to all; but it is *efficacious* — spiritually, savingly efficacious — *in you.* It was for you "especially" that he left his glory. It was for you "especially" that he was despised and rejected. It was for you "especially" that he entered into covenant with the Father. It was for you as a *sinner.* It was for you as a violator of his Law. It was for you as an enemy of God. It was for you as one who could neither make nor procure a recompense for your transgressions. But for his sacrifice there *never could* have been reconciliation between you and God. But for his sacrifice there never could have been a *respite* for you from the curse of the Law. But for his sacrifice there never could have been a hiding-place for your soul, or a fountain for the liquidation of your guilt. But for his sacrifice, your doom would have been sealed, your perdition would have been sure. There was no price, elsewhere, *sufficient* for your salvation. He came and made his sacrifice — for whom? For *you*. He came and paid the price — for whom? For *you;* for you, *who believe*. Just before he gave himself to death, he consecrated himself by prayer as the Lamb of God. He consecrated himself — for *you*. "Father," said he, "neither pray I for these alone, but for them also who shall *believe* on me through their word." And with *your* name upon the charter of Redemption; with *your* future faith full before his view; pointing the Father "specially" to the terrible record which would be made of *your* sins; with the precious and solemn prayer for *your* soul upon his lips; — he went away to the garden; he went out and trod the winepress; he went forth to shame, — to death, — to sacrifice.

O, yes! *you* were in his eye, my believing brother. *You* were in his eye; *you* were on his heart, — in that night of terror, — in that hall of judgment, — in that hour when God forsook him. He bore *your* griefs. He carried *your* sorrows. He was wounded for *your* transgressions. He was bruised for *your* iniquities. He was buffeted,—it was "specially" for *you.* He was mocked,—it was "specially" for *you.* He was reviled in the hour of his crucifixion,—it was "specially" for *you.* His soul was darkened, and stricken, and desolate, and crushed. The cry went forth from the Throne of thrones, "Awake, O sword! against my Shepherd, against the man that is my fellow!" And the response went up from the cross, "My God! my God!" And the blow was struck; the blood was poured out; the sacrifice was made; and all, and each and every part,—each drop of blood,—each cry,—each stripe,—was specially—"specially"—for *you.*

He made a *sure* provision for your pardon. He "*finished* the work which was given him to do." The Redemption was full. The price was enough. The Sacrifice was perfect; without spot,—without blemish. When he suffered and shed his blood, with you in his eye, with your name upon his lip, with your sins upon his soul, he *effected* Redemption. He laid the *only possible* foundation for your salvation; and he laid it broad, and deep, and sure. It was done *for* you expressly, and it was *enough* for you fully.

Estimate, now, the preciousness of the soul,

the greatness of your sins, the worth and the price of your redemption. Then, and not till then, can you estimate your debt to Christ for his suffering of death. Ye are redeemed! Ye are redeemed! But know ye, — *remember* ye, — "ye were not redeemed with corruptible things, as silver and gold, ... but with the precious blood of Christ, as of a lamb without blemish and without spot, ... manifest . . . . . *for you* who by him do believe in God."

Here is something more than you can weigh. Yet this is only a part of your indebtedness to Christ.

You are indebted to him for *personal grace.* What is this personal grace? Look and see. You did not choose Christ, but he chose you. The work of grace which has been wrought in you, *he* has wrought; he to whom "all things are delivered of the Father."

You were a wanderer from God, and he sought you. You were a stranger, and he found you. You were a sinner, and he hedged you about with the means of grace. You were a cumberer of the ground, ready and fit to be cut down; he plead for you, and cultured you. You were perverse, but he would not give you up. You were in all the filth of unpurged, unwashen, accumulated iniquity, but he would not pass you by. He came and pursued you, and beset you, and wrought upon you, and wrought in you by his Spirit.

Christian brethren, whence are ye brought? Whither are ye brought? What change has been made in you? in your condition? in your prospects? Where were you once? What were you? Where are you now? and what are you? Why! you "were far off" from God; "alienated and enemies in your mind by wicked works"; now "ye are made nigh." You were polluted,—you were polluted in every member and in every thought,—there was no good thing in you; you were under condemation. "*But* ye are washed, ye are sanctified, ye are justified in the name of our Lord Jesus Christ, and by the Spirit of our God." Ye "were children of wrath even as others"; but now are ye "children of the living God"; children of his dear love. Ye were heirs of perdition; but now are ye "joint heirs with Christ." Ye were poor bond-slaves, sold under sin; but now are ye "the Lord's freemen." Ye were "in the gall of bitterness"; but now ye drink of the waters of the river of life. Ye were "like the troubled sea when it cannot rest"; but now ye have been made to taste of peace. Ye were rushing onwards, blinded and deceived, in the road to the second death; but now ye are with your faces heavenward. You were upon the very brink of destruction, your "feet were upon slippery places"; but now you are upon a Rock of Safety, you are beneath a Refuge of Almighty Love. There was no bond of union, no oath of betrothal (Hos. ii. 19) between you and God; but now, from his love and care and covenant, "neither death, nor life, nor angels, nor principalities, nor powers, nor things present, nor things to come, nor height, nor depth, nor any other creature, shall be able to separate you."

You were poor. You had no surety of a single blessing. Your treasures were moth-eaten. The things which you loved most were taking to themselves wings. But now "all things are yours; whether Paul, or Apollos, or Cephas, or the world, or life, or death, or things present, or things to come; all are yours, and ye are Christ's, and Christ is God's."

What is there which is evil, and fearful, and accursing, which did *not* pertain to you? What is there which is good and precious, which is not now secured to you?

What has been wrought in you? *What* has been wrought for you? Resurrection! spiritual resurrection! Whence — whither — have ye been brought? "From darkness to light"! From bondage to liberty! From beggary to riches! From death to life! "From the power of Satan unto God"!

And it is *Christ's* work. It is *all* his work. It is his work, because he laid the foundation for it in his blood. It is his work, because he covenanted with the Father *for* you. It is his work, because he has overruled every influence, earthly and heavenly, human and divine, outward and inward, providential and spiritual, by which it has been accomplished. It is his work. It is *all* his. Ye "love him *because* he *first* loved you."

It is Christ's work. It is a wondrous work. It is a precious work. But — it is all a work of *grace*. It is of *pure* grace. It is of *free* grace. It is of *sovereign* grace. It has not been wrought because ye were good, for ye were evil; nor because ye were worthy, for you had no particle of good desert; nor because you had more claim to blessing than others, for both you and they had *no* claim. Christ has wrought it, not because he must, but because he would; not because in any sense he was compelled, but of his own free, sovereign pleasure — purely; not for your sakes, but for his own name's sake. (1 John ii. 12; Ephes. ii. 7.)

Look, — look, — my brother in covenant. See whereon you stand to-day! See to whom you are bound! See where and what you are! Look unto the rock whence you are hewn, and to the hole of the pit whence you are digged, — add this to the cost and the sureness of your Redemption, — and then scan the amount of your debt to Christ.

But this is not all. You are indebted to Christ for special and wonderful forbearance.

His forbearance toward those who believe not in him is wonderful indeed. But, if I mistake not, it is slight compared with his forbearance toward you and toward me.

O, my brother, what a story is that of our Christian discipleship! a story of unfaithfulness, of ingratitude, of inconstancy, of departure, of fluctuating love, of spiritual treacheries, the very mention of which should make us ashamed; a story at which heaven might shudder were it not a brilliant comment on the grace of God; such a story that it must drive us back — back — to despair, were it not for the measureless efficacy, the matchless sufficiency, of the blood of Christ.

Why! when we were washen in that blood of atonement; when Christ came to us and whispered, "Son, — daughter, — thy sins are forgiven, go in peace"; when he came to us in the midnight darkness of our conviction, as we stood pale and trembling at the foot of the mount that thundered and flashed and shook with tempests, and said, "It is I, be not afraid," — we said we would be his. We said so in secret places. We came to his altar and said so there. We made our vows in his sanctuary. We took upon us the seal of his covenant. We declared, — we published, — that to us he was the chief among ten thousand, and the one altogether lovely. * * * And how has it been with us since? Where have we been? What have we been? How have we kept our vows? What return have we made for his Redeeming Love? What return for his special, electing, renewing grace? What return for the precious hope of immortal life? What return for deliverance from the lashings of the Law, and the lashings of conscience? What return for our precious seasons of closet fellowship? What return! Why, — we forgot him! We *forgot* him! I say, — we FORGOT him! The thunders of the Law were hushed; the smart of our scourgings subsided; the flashing of the fire that burneth passed away; our wounds were healed, — yes! by *his* stripes, by *his* blood, — and we forgot our Deliverer!

The tempter spread his charms before us; the world smiled; subtle enticers begged us to *taste* the cup of enchantment; and we were snared, — we yielded, — we tasted. The smile of fleshly indulgence seduced us from the smile of Jesus Christ, and we plunged — with his seal upon us, with his vows upon us, with his blood upon us — amid the buzz and the tumult of worldly business and relationships. We put him, who brought us salvation, to open shame. We wounded him in the house of his friends. The love of our espousals has cooled. The fervor of our purpose has abated. We have been treacherous to our beloved. We have broken our vows. We have forgotten our purposes and our obligations.

Where have been our *fruits?* our *good* fruits? What have been our labors for Christ? What have been our self-denials for Christ? Where has been our spiritual-mindedness? Where has been the brightness of our piety? Who can *tell*—where? Who can *tell*—what?

And our neglects of duty,—how many? And our indulgences in sin,—how many? The occasions which we have given to others to despise spiritual religion,—how many? The times in which we have made our profession a by-word and a contempt,—how many?

Do you say that this picture is too dark for you? Do you doubt whether it be not overwrought? For *me*, my brother, it is not. I know it is not for me; and I verily *believe* it is not for *you*. I believe that by and by it will appear that this is not half the truth.

But enough of this. How has it been with our Lord all this while? Has *his* love cooled? No. Has *his* covenant-oath been forgotten? No. Have his purposes of grace and kindness faltered? No. No. Through the whole—he has loved us still. Through the whole—he has borne with us. He is *still* kind,—*still* gracious. He has watched for our return. His eye has followed us in all our wanderings. Every day,—every night,—in every hour of treachery,—in every scene of inconsistent indulgence,—he has been with us. All along, he has been shaping his providences, shaping his blessings, shaping and tempering and timing his chastisements, precisely and accurately for our good; busy, watchful, earnest, to make all things "work out for us an exceeding weight of glory." And now to-day, — it matters not where we are; it matters not what we are; it matters not how far we have gone in declension and apostasy and treachery; it matters not how low we have sunken in shame, — he is ready to receive us back again to his arms, to his love, to his fellowship, to his consolations, to his forgiveness.

O the forbearance, — the forbearance of Christ towards us! O the greatness of our debt to him for this!

But — his Redemption for you, — his special grace to you, with all its wonders, — and his forbearance, — these are only *items* in the account of his favors. I have said nothing of the precious works of his hands, — nothing of the bounteous ministrations of his providence, — nothing of how he has blessed you with health and with sickness, with abundance and with bereavement, with joy and with afflictions, — nothing of his gift of Hope, — nothing of the grace of his fellowship, — nothing of his ministrations for you in heaven, — nothing of the mission of angels which he has established for your protection and comfort, — nothing of the crown of glory, or the inheritance of bliss and love and perfect grace, which he keeps in store.

Come, brother, think of your debt to Christ; your *peculiar* debt. Think of the wonders he has wrought for you, and in you. Think of his sufferings. Think of his forbearance. Think of his ceaseless, precious favors ever since the day of your covenant. Remember — by the blood of your Ransom, by the agony of your Sacrifice, I adjure you to remember — these things; what you *were*, what you *are*. Remember *by* whom, and *through* whom, and *how* you are what you are. Remember the chains and the bondage, the darkness and the curse, the wormwood and the gall; the beauty and the preciousness of your dawning hope. Remember *Jesus Christ;* all that he *has* been to you; all that he *means* to be to you. Remember what he is doing. Your crown, he is shaping it. Your harp, he is tuning it. Your seat of princedom and of priesthood, (for "ye shall be kings and priests unto God,") he is preparing it. Remember, — "Sometime you were far off, an alien from the commonwealth of Israel, a stranger from the covenants of promise." *He* sought you. *He* found you.

He drew you. And now you "are made nigh by — *his* blood." Matchless — matchless — grace!

What are you going to render back for it? What are you going to *render back for* it? A little more indolence? A little more stupidity? A little more languid love? A little more backsliding? A little more sleep, and a little more slumber?

What! *you*, a redeemed one! redeemed by blood! by the Son of God! *You*, a subject of his transforming power! *You*, who "were dead in trespasses and sins"! *You*, "whom he hath quickened" by his sovereign grace!

Brother in covenant, *what are you going to do?* What *are* you going to render back to Christ? From henceforth, — from this moment, evermore, — what will you *render back* to Christ? Love for love? heart for heart? oath for oath? constancy for constancy? — *or not?*

See! the heaven-wide, amazing difference between what you *are* and what you *were!* Look at it. It is *your Redeemer's* work. Look. Say, — *will* you, — *will* you render back to him oath for oath, love for love, heart for heart, *henceforth*, — *or not?*

XII.

SERVICE THE REQUIREMENT OF CHRIST.

There are two opposite errors respecting the requirements of Christ which are common among those who have received his Gospel. The one is, that he requires only those duties which concern our social relations, — such as truth, honesty, kindness, gentleness; the other, that he requires some exercises of heart which are either so mystical that we cannot understand them, or so high and holy that we cannot yield them.

These, I say, are errors. The first results from a very narrow and worldly idea of the Christian religion; the other from an idea so attenuated, flighty, and vague, as to overlook and overfly those practical traits of piety which are its essential beauties. Both these errors are evils. They are each misconceptions of the Gospel. They are each entangled with false views of Christ. They each lead to respective errors in practice; drawing us away from that "holiness without which no man can see the Lord." I think of no one passage of Scripture having more appropriate reference to these errors than the simple injunction of our Saviour, that we should "take his yoke upon us." In this command are comprised, I conceive, all the requirements of Christ. If we do what he here enjoins, we are Christians. If we refuse, we are not Christians.

The directions of the Gospel are clothed in a variety of terms. Sometimes we are told "to repent"; sometimes, "to believe"; sometimes, "to come unto Christ." These several directions evidently involve each other; i. e. Faith is always hand in hand with Repentance, and with coming unto Christ. They are exercises of mind which cannot exist separately. So that it is a matter of indifference to which particular one the sinner is pointed, or with which particular one his eye is occupied; for, if he is persuaded to one, he does necessarily yield to all. It is so with the requirement that we should take upon ourselves the yoke of Christ. Whoever complies with it does, as a matter of course, comply with these other directions of the Gospel. And thus this one does truly cover the whole ground of Christian duty.

"Repent" is a plain command. So is "Believe." So is "Come unto me." And yet so much have men compassed these directions about with the clouds and mists of speculative theology, that the language "take my yoke" may gain more easy access to our understanding and conscience than, perhaps, any other exhortation of Christ. It is simple. It is direct. It is obviously and purely practical. It is difficult to understand how one *can* blunder respecting the nature of Christian virtue; it is difficult to understand how one *can* fall into the errors which I have named; it is difficult to understand how one *need* be kept from eternal life, — the wiles, and snares, and lies of Satan notwithstanding, —if this one command of Christ, so express, so simple, so practical, be kept before the mind.

The yoke has always been an emblem of service. Our Saviour, therefore, evidently calls upon us to enlist in his service; to hold ourselves, henceforth, subject to his direction; to acknowledge him openly and practically as our Master. The most superficial reader of the Bible cannot be ignorant that this is demanded by Christ of all whom he came to redeem. He claims the right to impose upon us such commands as he pleases, and to receive our obedience of those commands.

But what is it to render obedience to Christ's commands? What is it to take upon ourselves Christ's yoke? What is it to acknowledge him as our Master?

Do we do it when we sit down and cull from his statute-book one class of his directions for our reverence and adoption, and leave another class untouched, — unstudied, — uncared for, — unpractised, — dishonored? Am I a Christian just because I pray; just because I confess Christ at his table; just because, so far forth, my conduct happens to correspond with his commands, — when, all the while, I neglect a score of others? By no means. No more a Christian for doing this, than I should be a Jew for abhorring swine's flesh, or a Mussulman for refusing wine.

Well, — vary the question. Am I a Christian just because I am honest, or good-natured, or meek, or gentle, or of amiable feelings and deportment in my domestic life? just because, in these things, I chance to tally with the laws of Christ, — when, in fifty others, I pay no manner of regard to his laws? Again the answer is clear and prompt from every one who has half an eye to see, — By no means, — no more a Christian than a moral pagan is; no more than Satan is, when he steals the garb and apes the deportment of an angel of light.

Vary the question again. Am I a Christian just because I have passed through a certain amount, or a certain kind, of religious experience, — such as fears or compunctions, — or just because I have been, or am, subject to pleasurable religious excitements; when all the while I decline the practical injunctions of Christ? No. No.

Though a man does "make long prayers," he is no Christian if he "devour widows' houses." Though a man does pay "tithes of mint, anise, and cummin," he is no Christian if he "omit judgment, mercy, and faith." Though a man do "compass sea and land to make one proselyte," he is no Christian if he "make him twofold a child of hell." And though a man be "beautiful outwardly," — moral, sanctimonious, a very Daniel in the sight of men, — he is no Christian if there are excess and iniquity untouched, uncontrolled within. Prayer, receiving the eucharist, and baptism, do not make a man a Christian, if he be a knave. Neither do honesty, and sobriety, and truth, and amiableness, if he neglect the sacraments and prayer. Neither do devotion and religious ceremonies, if he neglect the practical duties of life. Nay, —

he may observe the whole, and yet be no Christian. He may observe the whole, and yet not take the yoke of Christ. He may observe the whole, and yet not obey Christ. But how so? Because, while Christ's commands touch upon these things, they go further. While they concern the outward life, they concern the heart. While they concern the heart, they concern its feelings both toward man and toward God; toward man and toward God alike and equally.

We are not serving Christ, — we are not acknowledging him as our Master, — when we choose one half of his rules and pass by the other half as though their words were like the babbling of a stream, or the whistling of the wind; no matter which half we choose, nor which half we reject. No, — no more than a soldier serves his country by shouldering his musket and taking the field, while he plots treason with the enemy. No more than a child serves his father in obeying him to-day, while he thwarts and defies him to-morrow.

Taking Christ's yoke signifies *serving* him. "Serving" him signifies holding ourselves subject to his directions. And his directions cover the whole field of actions; outward as well as inward, — inward as well as outward; toward

God as well as toward man, — toward man as well as toward God. This is its evident and comprehensive signification.

But, let it be observed, there is a peculiar significance in the command to "take Christ's yoke," to which we have not yet alluded. If we *do* adopt his Word as our rule of conduct; if we *do* set out, and go on, to render obedience to his commands; if we *do* undertake to regulate both life and heart, — our affections toward man and our affections toward God, — in the manner which he prescribes; after all, we may not serve *Christ* in what we do. We may be serving *ourselves* in our religion. We may rush to the commandments of the Gospel in a fit of fear and *merely* because we would be safe. We may turn to religion in a fit of ascetic disappointment, because the world has cheated us, or conscience has plagued us, and we want to get peace. Now if this is all, — I say, if this is *all;* for Christ does not forbid us to desire and seek our own good, — if this is *all* for which we undertake the duties of Christ's kingdom, we do but serve *ourselves* in our religion. Christ asks for something more. He requires us in all our religion to serve *him*. In other words, — he expects of us, that in all which we do we should seek *his interests* more than those of any other one. He expects of us to be *more* desirous of his honor, of his pleasure, of the prosperity of his kingdom, of the triumph of his grace, than we are for our own profit, either here or hereafter. He expects, evidently, — not indeed that we should be careless of ourselves; not indeed that we should not pant for our own salvation, — but that, while we adopt his laws, while we take his yoke, the *great* reason why we do so should be our love and gratitude *to him.*

It may be that, as your eye glances over these pages, you are conscious that you are not, spiritually, a Christian. It may be, also, that you are really desirous, and that you even *seek*, to become a Christian. You are convinced, perhaps, of your peril; convinced, perhaps, of your exceeding guilt as a sinner against God; but you are benighted, — you are perplexed. You have sought, you say, but you have not found; you have desired, but you have not obtained. Perhaps all this is true. Yes, — and something more is true. You have tried to meet the Gospel's directions. You have *tried* "to repent," — i. e. you have tried to urge yourself up to a certain pitch of emotion about your sins; but you could not reach it; after all, repentance would not come. And you have *tried* "to believe," — i. e. you have tried to kindle within yourself such feelings toward Christ as he commands; but after all, the fire would not burn, — your heart is dead, and cold, and icy. And now you think that there is something mysterious, — something inexplicable, — something beyond your reach, — in this matter of becoming a Christian. Or you say, that "you must sit down and wait, — idle, passive, patient, — until God comes (if he shall please to come) and *make* you a Christian; that you cannot regenerate yourself; that *God* must do that; that if he does not, you must perish."

But — *what* have you sought? For *what* have you tried? To regenerate yourself? To *make* yourself repent? But that is something which you cannot do. That is something over and above your duty. *That* is something which you cannot find in the directions of Christ. Your Saviour does not tell you to do what only God can do. Your labor has indeed been in vain, *because* you have mistaken your duty — utterly.

There is another thing to be considered, too. Christ does not insist upon *perfect* obedience. That is to say, — he does not require that you shall keep entirely and uniformly every one of his commandments in order to *pardon and acceptance.* If he did, the Gospel — the way of salvation by Christ — would be no better than the Law; for the Gospel is as broad as the Law. Christ "came not to destroy the Law, but to fulfil." He does not, "through grace, make void the Law" in the matter of one jot or one tittle; contrarywise, he "establishes the Law." And if you have thought that you must be *pure* in heart and *pure* in life *before* you could be a Christian; and if you have aimed at this as *the means* of becoming a Christian, — there again you have mistaken what Christ requires; there again you have "spent your labor in vain."

What, then, *must* you do? Just keep in mind what you are *not* to do. Just keep in mind that you are not to do *God's* work; that you are not to regenerate your own heart; that you are not to make yourself perfect; *and* that you are not to sit still, in the midst of your tremendous perils and responsibilities, doing *nothing*, — and I will tell you. In one word, — *take Christ's yoke.* Begin, — *begin* his service. Go to your closet, — go out under the vault of heaven, — go anywhere you will, and make a covenant with Christ, that whatsoever he tells you to do, that you *will do.* And, then, begin and *do it.*

Now, my beloved, but bewildered, fellow-sinner, how simple a thing this is! There is no metaphysical mummery about it. There is no clashing, no jargon, of inconsistencies in this. There is no mist and darkness. It is sunshine; sunshine because it is clear, — sunshine because, if you come to it, it will cheer your soul, it will gladden your eye. It will warm you with the glow of life that angels feel. It will reveal to you the glories which an angel sees. It will move your heart to such melody as an angel makes in heaven. Come, — away from your halting-place; away from that miserable position where doubts and fancies becloud and scare you like the mists and howlings of a tempest. Come, — take the yoke of Christ upon you. This is all you have to do. Begin his service. *Make yourself over* to him, — body and soul.

But you ask, — Is this all? Is this Scriptural? Must I not first "repent"? must I not first "believe"? must I not first "come unto Christ"? My dear reader, — *no.* Take Christ's yoke. Adopt his service. *This* is — "repentance." *This* is — "faith." *This* — is "coming unto Christ." And, all the while, you have been trying after faith and repentance just as though they were something different. And that has been your snare. That has been your stumbling-block. And if you cleave to that, you will be bound hand and foot by your own doctrines; you will be dashed to pieces, and ground to powder, by your own devices.

Your path is plain. Your duty is simple, however much it may involve. Take the yoke of Christ. *Serve* him. Serve *him.* Begin to-day. Begin now.

But perhaps you belong to a different class. You may think yourself to be something in Christ's estimation, when in truth you are nothing. You may call yourself a Christian, — you may think yourself good, — while it is not so. Test yourself by the Word. Test yourself by the simple command which we have pointed out. Test yourself by these, — for by these you must *be tested.*

You — are crying to your soul, — "Peace"; because you have been the subject of religious impressions, or have experienced certain religious pleasures. You flatter yourself on *this* ground that you are a Christian. At the same time, you neglect prayer; or you neglect the sacraments; or you neglect your social duties;

or, your temper; or, your tongue. You take no more heed to some score or two of Christ's commandments than though they had no existence. Well, — *are* you a Christian? *Are* you Christ's? *Are* you subject to his direction? What! when you throw his directions to the winds — every day? Impossible.

But *you* — are one who goes current in the church for a pattern of piety. You come up promptly to visible religious duties. You make prayers. You talk to the wicked. You rebuke your brethren. You ride upon the top wave of religious enterprises. You give alms to the poor. You are what is called "an active Christian"; no drone, — no sleeper. But, — my brother, — what of it? Here is indeed something which looks like a corner of the garment of piety, — but what of it? Have you the whole? Have you — the garment? How is it with you in your ordinary business? Do you aim to conduct all your contracts, all your negotiations, all your payments, — just as Christ would have you? How is it with you in your private relations? Do you strive to behave *at home* as Christ would have you? as a parent, — as a child, — as a husband, — as a wife? How is it with your *temper?* Do you bring that under the rules of Christ?

How is it with your *tongue?* Do you bring *that* under the rules of Christ? Now if you do pass over *these* things; if you do neglect to guide yourself by Christ's rules in *these;* with all your prayers, — with all your religious zeal, — with all your high reputation for piety, — you are "as sounding brass, as a tinkling cymbal." You are not yielding your neck to the yoke of Christ.

But I think I hear another say, — "Right, but *I* pay my tithes; *I* do justice; *I* love mercy; *I* am exemplary and scrupulous in the street, and at home." Yes, — yes, — but do you "*walk* — humbly — *with your God*"? Heart and life echo to the claims of neighbor and kindred. You wrong no man. You are the light and the life of your family circle. You have the orphan's love and the widow's blessing. But — in the name of your soul — are you *a Christian?* Where is your piety *toward God?* Do heart and life echo to *his* claims, as well as to your neighbor's? Do you strive against *inward* sins? Remember, — the commands of Christ sweep over the *whole* of your relations. They point you to *God* as well as to man; to your *heart* as well as to your life.

To *all* who are living in the neglect of any class, or of any *one*, of Christ's commands, I say, — Take heed. You — *Christians*! You — good men! good women! good children! What! when you refuse the yoke of Christ! when you do *not* subject yourselves to his commands! when you adopt one half, and reject one half! No, — no. If you refuse his yoke, if you decline his *service*, Christ is not your Master. And then, — O the foundation of your soul! it is a quicksand! The fabric of your hope, — it is a bubble! With all your morality, — with all your religion, — with all your religious experience, — if you take not Christ's yoke, your bright visions of salvation will vanish, like the mists of the morning, when the light of another world shall reveal the nakedness of your soul.

"Be not deceived; God is not mocked." Are you *Christ's*? Do you *wear his yoke?* This, — *this* is the question.

XIII.

THE RESULTS OF THE CHRISTIAN'S AFFLICTIONS.

He who loves and trusts God derives peculiar satisfaction from the thought that all events, without exception, are under God's control. He loves to dwell upon this truth, especially when he observes the intricacy, and the mystery, and the seeming confusion and contradiction of things around him. A thousand facts transpire, whose reasons, whose tendency, whose righteousness, he can in no wise understand. But it is *enough* for him to know, that "not a sparrow falleth to the ground without his Heavenly Father." Nay, — a thousand things transpire which seem positively productive of evil; the wicked prevail, — the Truth is ineffectual, — a host of inventions spring up in the hearts of those who care not for God. But it is *enough* for such a a believer that "the wrath of man shall praise God, and that the remainder of wrath he will restrain."

But let us select, for special inspection, a particular branch of the general truth of God's universal superintendence. While he is controlling all events, *he is controlling them for the good of those who trust him.*

Yes; this "we *know*, that all things work together for good to them that love God; — *all* things, — the greatest and the least, — the brightest and the darkest, — far and near, — past, present, future; *all* things, — plenty and famine, — health and pestilence, — every revolution and convulsion of governments, — every discovery and invention of man, — the working of every press, and the labor of every engine, — all are under the sway of God, and they all serve God; not only for the ultimate triumph of his grace, but for the full and perfect joy of all his saints.

If *all* things work together for good to them who love God, then surely the troubles of life do. Every thing which befalls them is ordered in love. Every thing which causes them grief is timed and measured to them in tender mercy, — *every thing;* whether the suffering and departure of wife, husband, children; or the unkindness, or treachery, or brutality of those whom they have trusted; or pecuniary reverses; or poverty; or the most transient difficulty of common life. If we love God, each and all are ordered for our good, and productive of our good.

Formal proof of this is needless. It is distinctly declared in the Holy Scriptures, and has been abundantly illustrated by the experience of the whole Church. Let me simply specify, for the consideration of my reader, some of the more prominent benefits which flow to God's people through the trials of their pilgrimage.

They who love God, love to go to him. They love prayer. They love that intercourse which is sustained between the soul and God at the mercy-seat. They love it at all times. But at no time does the Christian go to God with such eagerness as when he is in trouble. When the heart is aching and bleeding,—when it throbs with grief, almost to bursting, — O, how good that refuge! How good the overshadowing of the mercy-seat! It is as grateful for him to go there when he is worried with cares, or dangers, or bereavements, as for the hunted deer to hide himself in the depths of the forest and to cool himself in its living fountains; as grateful as for the frighted bird to alight safely in its quiet nest; as grateful as for the wearied, terror-stricken child to leap to its mother's arms. It is as grateful; it is as natural. And there, — before God, — in the day of his adversity, it is with a full, and fervent, and eloquent heart, that the child of God pours out his troubles and his wants. There is no coldness, no formality, about his devotions then. There is no want of words, no stammering, upon his tongue. He comes under the impulse of a beating heart. He comes in earnest. He comes with boldness. He *plunges* into the fountain. He lays hold upon the Almighty arm *with his whole strength.* He *must*, — for to none else can he go. He *must*, — for none else can know his heart's bitterness. He *must*, — for nothing else can suit his case; nothing else can touch the spot of pain within him. And thus he is brought into *close*, *earnest* communion with God. He throws himself, as it were, upon the very arms of his Father; lays his throbbing head upon his very bosom; lifts up his tearful eyes and drinks in the very light of his countenance.

A little bird sitting amid the foliage of a tree is frightened by some noise beneath. He flies to a higher branch. Again, — and he leaps to a higher. Again, — to the topmost bough. Again, — and he soars away toward heaven. Just so with the Christian; *just so.* Disturbed by the commotions, and terrors, and troubles of things *beneath*, his first impulse is to leap *upward.* Again, — to ascend higher and still higher; and at last, to fly away toward heaven, — toward his God, — where, for the time, no distress or adversity can reach him; to the sure place of refuge, the free expanse of undisturbed communion with his Father.

I need not explain *how* this is; though to do so would be very simple. It is sufficient that such is the fact.

But there is another natural effect of worldly trouble upon the Christian. The same spiritual instinct which impels him, in a day or an hour of darkness, to flee to God for fellowship, also impels him to look about him and examine afresh the tokens of God's character and the features of God's government. *God* has smitten him. *God* has made him drink the cup of bitterness. This is his first thought. But what is his second? To see if he cannot find some argument in the grief which has befallen him wherewith to impeach the character and government of Him who has smitten? No. He casts about him, instantly, to strengthen his faith. He wants to gather together the glowing evidences of God's goodness. He wants to bring them before his eye in one blazing constellation of beauty and glory. He wants to gather them together in one living assemblage to pour their melting eloquence upon his heart anew, so that his spontaneous response shall be, — "Though thou slay me, yet will I trust in thee; though the fig-tree shall not blossom, neither shall fruit be in the vines; the labor of the olive shall fail, and the fields shall yield no meat; the flock shall be cut off from the fold and there shall be no herd in the stalls, yet I will rejoice in the Lord and joy in the God of my salvation."

And thus he brings up before himself the character and the government of God as they are declared in the Word, as they are interpreted in the mystery of the cross of Christ, in Providence, in Nature, in all things. He finds that they abide the scrutiny. Nay, the closer he inspects the more he finds to admire, the more to adore, the more to trust. He finds that the very smartings of his fleshly state have brought him to clearer and dearer views of the God of his fathers, — the adorable God of his covenant.

I have only to add on this point, that the natural and necessary influence of these two things — communion with God, and the inspection of his character and government — is to quicken the exercise of every Christian grace. In other words, to lead the Christian to new faith, to new love, to new hope, to new consecration. Here are nearer and clearer views of God gained under the operation of trials. A new view of God, a new season of communion, are only new incentives to the gracious affections of the Christian's heart. But these affections grow *by exercise.* They are strengthened, matured, perfected, *by action,* just like any other affection or power. And thus, while afflictions drive the Christian to the resources of God, and bring him to more intimate acquaintance with God, and excite anew his affections toward God, they are — plainly — special, efficacious, precious means of his growth in holiness.

Another benefit which I specify as accruing to God's people from their afflictions is — spiritual comfort.

The Apostle Paul, who not only wrote under the inspiration of the Holy Spirit, but from the teachings of his own experience also, holds such language as this: "Blessed be God, even the Father of our Lord Jesus Christ, the Father of mercies, and the God of all comfort, who *comforteth* us in *all* our tribulation; . . . . for as the sufferings of Christ abound in us, so our *consolation* also aboundeth by Christ." And he also says to the Corinthian Christians, "Our hope of you is steadfast, *knowing* that, as ye are partakers of the sufferings, so shall ye be also of the consolation."

One who is not a child of God by adoption, when *he* meets with trouble, receives no spiritual ministrations from above. His heart is shut against them. Unbelief sits at the door, effectually keeping away every angel of mercy which a God of comfort sends. Affliction either preys upon his life, and makes the whole world to him a world of gloom, or he drowns his trouble in the waves of business or pleasure. But God has ways of comforting his afflicted children which the world neither know nor understand. While the heart of the believer, in trouble, turns itself toward Him, He turns himself toward it. While the child flees to the Father, the Father smiles and embraces the child. While the cry of grief is uttered to Him, the ministration of Divine grace is poured out. It is as when the Spirit of God moved upon the face of the waters. It is as the voice of Jesus upon the sea, "Peace, be still"; as the voice of the Master to his disciples, "It is I; be not afraid."

Such is the work which God effects for his people in the days of their tribulation. He gives them "the oil of joy for mourning; the garment of praise for the spirit of heaviness." He softens the anguish of their grief. He sweetens its bitterness. He tempers its sharpness. He soothes its tumults. And after the first gust of agitation is spent, he sheds abroad in the heart a spirit so like that of angels, that you can see there the plastic influence of the same hand which has strung the harps, and given the peace, of heaven.

I thank God that in my brief life I have seen such proofs of his grace; that I have seen the difference which he makes between the righteous and the wicked in their times of trouble. I have witnessed many scenes of distress. I have seen a godless man, in convulsive agony, beside the grave of some buried hope. I have seen his body and soul almost riven asunder by the tempest; the world — his darling world — black as very midnight; and his heavens sheeted with one vast cloud of comfortless indignation. I have watched him when thus stricken to the earth; and in a fit of reckless anguish he has gathered himself up, and then launched out, without a single dispensation of God's mercy to his soul, upon the wild waters of worldly care and diversion, — that he might *forget* the day and the bitterness of his affliction; that he might *sear* and *harden* the heart which could find no comfort.

But I have seen others into whose souls the iron had also entered, — who had felt it as keenly too, — placid and gentle under the stroke; "behaving themselves and quieting themselves as a child that is weaned of his mother." The blast had passed over them, and they had bent beneath it; but they arose again, and, like the bruised reed, struck forth their roots the more eagerly for the moisture which the blast had scattered, and looked upward the more earnestly for warmth and brightness to the very heavens whence came their tribulation. Yes, — I have seen them brighter Christians; better, — happier. I have heard their tremulous hymns of praise to Him who had tried them. I have heard them testify, that "as the sufferings of Christ had abounded in them, so their *consolation* also had abounded by Christ."

But there is a benefit which accrues *here-*

after to God's people from their worldly troubles.

The Psalmist seems to express in very marked language the idea which I would here present. He says, " Make us *glad* according to the days wherein thou hast afflicted us, and the years wherein we have seen evil. Let thy *work appear* unto thy servants, and thy glory unto their children." As though he was expecting future joy in precise *proportion* to past affliction; as though he was expecting that joy to come in connection with — as the result of — those afflictions. Nay, more, — as though he was expecting that God's " work " *in* those afflictions would hereafter be all unravelled; the mystery, the reasons, the kindness, the operation of it all made plain ; and that thus the "*glory*" of God in his dispensation of trials would be made to " appear," not only to the afflicted, but to others also.

The future world (the Bible warrants us in saying it) is to be a world of revelation. The great map of God's dealings is to be unrolled, and we are to study it and understand it. We are to trace out the hidden mysteries of Redemption ; the untold sufferings of Christ upon the cross ; the overruling influence of God in all the convulsions, and sins, and miseries of a ruined world; the precise bearings of all which God has here brought about upon the grand result of the world's regeneration. We shall have made clear to us all the particulars of the world's history, and see how God's finger was secretly and discreetly arranging and managing the whole. We shall see their reasons; their influences; how they have all moved on, under the control of Him who ruleth over all, harmoniously, admirably, unerringly; each tributary (whether designingly or undesigningly, willingly or unwillingly), each tributary, in its time and measure, to the production of those ends for which God in goodness and righteousness has made and upheld the world. Of course there will be unrolled before us the particulars of our *personal* histories. The child of God will review his career step by step, point by point, from the cradle onward. Forgotten events, — events at the very time of their occurrence almost unnoticed, — all will be brought up before him in heaven, and all their reasons and their subtle influences disclosed. The bearings of every connection and relation in life, and of their character, and of their rupture, will stand out before him with perfect distinctness. He will see how God led him into them all, and arranged them all, and timed them all, and managed them all. He will see also how they served, each one in its own place and measure, to secure his salvation, to mould and perfect his spirit in the likeness of God. The necessity of his *afflictions*, therefore, will appear. He will see their gentleness, their wisdom, their perfect fitness to his wants, their productive influence upon his heavenly glory. He will see how each one *did* something in the precious work of attuning his heart to the heavenly song, — of fitting his brow for the heavenly crown. He will see how every secret sigh, and tear, and weariness, was allotted to him for the express purpose of his preparation for glory; and how they wrought out that purpose; and how for that purpose they could not have been spared. And as he traces out all these particulars, — as the "work of God appears" herein, — how like a flood will be the disclosure of God's wondrous glory! How enrapturing will be the demonstration of God's tender mercy, of his accurate loving-kindness, in the whole! *This* is the fountain of the "gladness" of the saints, — the outflowing revelation of the goodness and holiness of Him who sitteth on the throne; of Him whom they love and adore. And as each specific trouble of their weary pilgrimage comes up before them with its interpretation, and as each interpretation thereof elicits a new radiance from the character of God, so will a new thrill of blissful emotions inspire the saint who sees, and a new anthem of praise from his burning lips will swell upward unto Him who hath redeemed by blood

> "It is the Lord whose matchless skill
> Can from afflictions raise
> Matter eternity to fill
> With ever-growing praise."

Thus most truly, most emphatically, most wondrously, will the saints be "made glad" precisely "according to the days wherein God has afflicted them, and the years wherein they have seen evil." Thus most wondrously are their present afflictions working together for their good.

When you go out at the opening of the morning, the dews lie beneath your feet so pure, so fresh, so brilliant, that you might almost think "an angel had scattered pearls from heaven" to cheer you with a sweet token of his unseen ministry, or with a pure memorial of his own home. But they are gone. They have gathered themselves together in the cloud, and come back to you with thunder and lightning and tempest. They veil the light of the sun and fill you with agitation. But you look again, and behold! there they are, set before you in all the glory of the bow of promise stretching itself over the heavens, and again filling you with wonder and gladness, — again displaying to you the goodness of God.

Just so the worldly beauties in which the Christian delights are ravished from him; and there gather about him the clouds of distress and affliction. But lo! when this is finished, a glory is revealed from the very sources of his disappointment brighter than the blessing of the morning. In the very events which ministered his affliction he shall behold a display of God's glory yielding him infinite compensation for the bitterness of his trial.

Times of trouble are times of honesty. Then men act without art. The prevailing temper of the spirit is developed. The lover of the world will turn to the world for relief. The lover of God, to God. When the heart most feels its weakness and dependence, then it yearns most sensibly after that in which it trusts. And never does it feel its weakness and dependence more than in the days of its tribulation. If, now, it is true that afflictions work together for good to them that love God and if it is true that special intercourse with God and special comforts are — to such — the sure fruits of afflictions, then it is plain that they who experience these blessings love God, and that they who do not experience them do not love him.

Does a man in the hour of sorrow betake himself to the throne of grace? Does he go there in the spirit of confidential fellowship? Does he throw himself upon God with the spirit of a sorrowing, affectionate, trustful child? Does he find that the hour of trouble is an hour when he cries, "Abba, Father," with unwonted emotion? when his soul seems melted within him by the lively fervor of his secret communion? Does he thus *grow in grace?*

Does he find that there is an unseen arm buoying him up amid the billows? that there is a soothing balm upon his wounds? that there seems to be another fountain opened within him of peace and quietness mingling with the fountain of his grief? Does he find that "the secret of the Almighty is with him"? and the witness of the Spirit? and a sweet concord of thoughts and feelings and affections blending themselves with the decrees and allotments of God? Does he thus find *comfort from* God?

Surely that man must *love* God. Surely there must be a medium of communication, a bond of union, between him and God, which cannot exist without love.

Again, — does a man go through trouble without fleeing to the mercy-seat? or, if he goes there, is it without nearness of access? Does his affliction excite him to no exercise of trust in God, or of the spirit of adoption? Does his heart ache and throb, and ache and throb without consolation? Is his grief *exhausted* rather than *soothed?* Is he conscious that there is something which might befit his case which he has not? that there is a spot within him which no balm as yet has reached? Is it thus evident that he gets no good, either of grace or of comfort, from his trouble? How plain it is, — how very plain, — if the testimony of Scripture is true, that that man does not love God. Why! either there is an error of doctrine in the Bible, or there is an error in his heart. Either there is an error of doctrine in the Bible, or *he* is in an error if he thinks that he loves a holy God.

Perhaps *you* have been bowed under the rod of your Heavenly Father. You have buried children or parents, husband or wife, brother or sister. Many a cord which has wound tightly about you has been torn asunder. Many a melancholy breach has been made in the circle of your domestic affections. The arrows of the Almighty have entered deep into your spirit. Go back now, and call up the memory of your wounds. Bring to mind the seasons of your by-gone griefs. Did they do you *good?* Did they impel you to God? Did they urge you to those exercises of heart which are the graces of the Holy Spirit? Did they prove to you seasons of consolation? seasons when the voice of God, and the name of God, and the promises of God, were life and spirit to you? And now, as you open your wounds afresh, — as you think of the love and endearment of those who lie waiting for you in the grave, — what is the influence thereof upon you? Fresh grief, — fresh tears, — I know. But what is the influence otherwise? Do they do you good *now?* With the memory of your bereavements, does there also steal over your agitated heart something like the light of God's countenance? something like the subduing, tranquillizing influence of the Holy Spirit? Or was it different with you when the rod smote you? And is it different now?

One thought more. We are born to trouble. Go through life without it, we cannot. This world is not our home. It is not our rest. And even those who, "in their *lifetime*, received *their* good things," bear many a burden; meet many a bereavement; give up many a darling blessing before they go down to their graves. Are you "without God in the world"? However bright your prospects, however strong the towers of your expectations, however sanguine your worldly hopes, you will find them all changed. Your prospects will grow dark. Your towers will crumble, piecemeal, to their foundations. Your hopes will fade away and depart, like the hope of the hypocrite, like the giving up of the ghost. Take to your bosom a companion for your journey; the tie which binds you to her is like the spider's web. Rejoice in the children around your board; death covets them for their very loveliness, and spreads his toils to catch them. If you live to the full age of man, you will part with many a worldly comfort; you will follow in the funeral train of many whom you love; you will feel many an arrow enter your heart. Nay, it may be that, when you come to stand upon the last limit of your pilgrimage, you will stand there like the tree of the forest whose fellows have fallen around it; alone, — blighted; to mock, by the decrepitude and imbecility and friendlessness of old age, the pride and glory and expectation of man. And then must come the last day of your distress, of your weakness, of your necessity; the day when you must go to meet your misdeeds and your God.

It will be a bitter thing for you if you encounter the successive evils of life, and get *no good* from them. It will be hard for you to bury your worldly blessings, and part with your worldly hopes, if with these afflictions you get no blessing. If the seasons of your troubles do not impel you to God to let out your heart before him like a child; if they do not quicken you to the work of searching "the unsearchable riches of Christ"; if they do not prove to you the occasions and the channels of God's comforting ministrations; then it will be terribly hard to endure them; it will be indeed a weary thing to live and a bitter thing to die. And this will be your lot, — this *must* be your lot, — if you do not turn unto God. Sanctified afflictions are the portion of those only who *love* God; of "them who are the called according to his purpose."

Now, then, there is a distinct and thrilling

argument in every contingency of life, in every earthly peril which besets you. There is a voice speaking to you from every point of hope and promise which is before you, pleading with you to enter into covenant with God, so that — upon whatsoever spot of life you may happen to stand, amid whatever desolations and griefs you may happen to be cast — the Spirit of God shall be with you there for your comfort and sanctification; and the angels of God, with their affectionate ministrations; — so that, however wide and drear the wilderness where you may happen to pitch your tent, the grace of God shall make it bud and blossom as the rose; — so that, however fearful the fire into which perchance you may be thrown, it shall purge you to the beauty and glory of an angel of light.

I beseech you, then, by the mercies of the Lord; by the mercies which he is able and willing to dispense to you in the days of your coming want; by all the necessity and the piteous helplessness of a soul when it is stricken by the hand of God; that you present yourself unto him a living sacrifice, soul and body. Give him your heart. Give him your love. Give him your confidence. Give him your fellowship. Else he will never give you his confidence, nor his fellowship, nor his love. Else he will leave you — he must — to buffet with the surges of your adversities alone, — comfortless. Else he will never turn them to the profit of your soul. Else he will make them interpreters of himself before your eyes hereafter, not to your joy and glory, but to your shame and everlasting contempt. Else you will go down to your grave and to your retribution, accountable for all the *offered* comforts of God, and for all the lessons of your days of affliction.

THE END.